FROM
LAND ᴛᴏ MOUTH

UNDERSTANDING
THE FOOD SYSTEM

BREWSTER KNEEN

Second Edition

NC Press Limited
Toronto

Design: Cathleen Kneen
Cover Art: Ricardo Ramirez

Canadian Cataloguing in Publication Data

Main entry under title:

From land to mouth

Bibliography: p.
Includes index.
ISBN 1-55021-085-8

1. Food supply – Political aspects.   2. Food industry and trade –
Political aspects.   3. Agriculture and state. I. Title.

HD9000.6.K54 1993   338.1'9   C89-093497-5

We would like to thank the Ontario Arts Council, the Ontario Publishing Centre, the Ontario Ministry of Culture, Tourism and Recreation, the Canada Council, and the Government of Canada, Department of Communications for their assistance in the publication of this book.

New Canada Publications, a division of NC Press Limited, Box 452, Station A, Toronto, Ontario, Canada, M5W 1H8.

Printed and bound in Canada

ACKNOWLEDGEMENTS

My thanks to all those whose response to the first edition encouraged me to do a second, including both my children. And again I must thank my critic, editor and wife, Cathleen, for her support and editorial assistance.

My thanks to the Ontario Arts Council, as well, for their support of this second edition.

Rose Janson's crucial and creative assistance made the first edition possible. It was dedicated to the memory of my Grade 10 English teacher, "Jiggs" Reardon. He persisted in impressing on me the importance of language and the necessity of thinking for oneself, not simply articulating the dominant culture. I hope this book will carry on his commitment and influence.

CONTENTS

PREFACE

THE FOOD SYSTEM AND ME

In the early 1960s when I lived along the Hudson River in New York State, there were numerous vistas where one could see veritable flotillas of rusting freighters anchored side by side. These retired merchant ships were storing surplus grain. I hardly wondered about the irrationality of it all in those days. I'm not sure I even knew exactly where the grain was grown. Scavenging discarded fruit in small-town farmer's markets as I hitch-hiked through the U.S.A. in the summertime did not strike me as irrational either. The surplus was taken for granted. If I could make use of what others had picked over, so much the better for me.

Years later, with small children, we were driving through the state of Maine on holiday. We were hungry and came upon what looked like a fair place to eat our picnic lunch. Then we noticed the prolific blueberries, and thought we would try some for dessert. We were quite taken aback by the angry shouts from the woman living next to this field of scrub. Where we came from, blueberries had always been wild 'surplus'. It was a number of years before I, too, would shout angrily at the trespassers stealing *my* berries in Nova Scotia.

At the age of 24 I went abroad to study. When my money was running out, I was still not ready to return home. I was determined to hold out until I had really sorted out what my convictions were about the world and what were those I had been indoctrinated with as a youth. By the time I did return home I had bald patches in my beard and on my scalp. I had no idea what was wrong with me, and I found out that neither did the medical profession in a fair-sized industrial and university city of New England. I was told to see a psychiatrist, a dermatologist, and so on. With no diagnosis, I went to visit my uncle, a country doctor. It took him about 15 seconds to observe and comment, Malnutrition!

Years later, in Cuba, we were part of a group visiting a small plantation. The farmer was lavish with his samples of oranges, grapefruit, coconuts, and everything else. Most of the group were country people and were at ease with the hospitality. The city girl felt compelled to suggest we take up a collection to pay the farmer. We laughed. The farmer would not have been pleased if we had walked along and helped ourselves, but his pleasure was in sharing the fruit of his labour.

There was very little eating out in my family. It was not my parents choice for entertainment and later I did not have the money to spend on fancy eating. I do remember banquets, however. At a work camp in Yugoslavia in 1957 (it was very much a country then) I was part of an International Brigade that included a number of Poles. Since I had been designated the leader of a motley bunch of Non-Socialist Country youth, I was a 'delegate' to the celebration of the Polish national day. This was a mid-day feast of Polish salami, fruits, and vodka that the Poles had brought with them for the occasion. I think it was the first feast I had ever attended, and the vulgarity I experienced in that celebration made an indelible impression on my Presbyterian consciousness.

Nearly thirty years later we held a feast of our own on our farm. After raising lambs for others for about 12 years we decided it was high time we tried one. So I celebrated my 50th birthday a year early with a whole lamb roasted on a spit, Greek style, with all of our sheep farmer friends and others attending. The next morning all we could find were the scattered bones and empty bottles. I said to myself, "Why did I wait so long to do that?"

It was on my 37th birthday that we took formal title to our farm in Nova Scotia. It was not a going concern at the time. Like me, the fellow we bought it from had not been a farmer, and he seemed to be as short on common sense as he was on financial resources. If I brought anything to the farm, it was common sense, along with my Christian faith, love of Creation, and a sensuous enjoyment of hard physical work. Neither my wife nor I had any farm experience or agricultural training. Some said this was to our advantage. Our children were three and five years old at the time.

We moved from Toronto to Nova Scotia as adults seeking greater integrity in our lives and a non-academic understanding of how capitalism functions in the hinterland, the Third World. I knew the theory and when we left Toronto I felt I knew as much as I needed to about how the economy works for the metropolis. It was how it worked on the hinterland, the other end of the system, that I needed to know.

By the time we left Nova Scotia 15 years later, in 1986, I felt I probably knew more than I really wanted to about the culture of the hinterland. The struggle against the continual drain of human and natural resources to feed the voracious appetite of the Metropolis, its bankers and its elite, had worn me down. Struggling to overcome the fatalism and the opportunism of a colonial culture was equally wearing.

When we moved we did not intend to farm. My aim was simply to get involved in primary production. As it happened we bought a farm, and on that farm were cattle and calves, a semblance of machinery and buildings, and an incredibly beautiful environment. It was July, and the previous owner was starting to make the hay, late. There was little to do but carry on. So we made the hay, such as it was and the machinery would allow, and we put it in the century-old barn, only to discover that the roof leaked badly. So between chasing cattle and repairing fences, with the help of a new neighbour or two I put a new roof on the barn.

Fifteen years later we were still making hay, but we weren't chasing livestock thanks to my Border Collie partner and our pioneering use of high power New Zealand electric fencing. We had sold the cattle some years earlier, at the endless bottom of what was called 'the beef cycle', after building up our sheep flock. By the time we left we had built three new barns and improved much of the land. We were also working three other old farms, farms that had once supported their own families, for better or for worse, and importing and selling sheep fencing and supplies.

That first year we tried to learn all we could from books, other farmers, and people like our Ag Rep (agricultural representative, or extension agent). Right from the start, with no experience or training, we realized that we would have to sort out the wisdom from the ideology and propaganda. We discovered this when we consulted with our Ag Rep about what we should be growing. His (the Department of Agriculture's) line at that time was "corn". Now, the land we had started to farm was glacial till in central Nova Scotia. We didn't need to be too smart to realize that there were neither the right soil conditions nor enough heat units where we were to even dream of growing corn, except sweet corn in the garden. But corn was 'on' that year in the program of the Department of Agriculture. This was the beginning of my questioning of agricultural policy.

During that first year, and every year after that, I learned more about policy and policies in agriculture. I found out that, in common language, policies referred essentially to the subsidy programs offered by the government. The total available subsidies constituted policy. That they might have contradictory consequences was less important than the fact that given the level of farm incomes, they were effective in shaping agriculture.

Over time, I came to understand how these policies did make sense from a particular perspective. That perspective is one of the things this book is about. It was not primarily a practical perspective, but an ideological commitment. It reflected the uncritical acceptance of industrialization and concentration, the substitution of capital for labour and the reduction of mixed farming to a specialized aspect of a larger food production system. This included machinery, seed and chemical companies, government advisors and corporate buyers. We farmed during the period when Eugene Whelan, as Minister of Agriculture, helped define farming as one aspect of the 'Agri-food' sector.

So we learned about policy as we added up the policies and observed the direction they would take us. We learned about the

Market Economy as we tried to sell first our beef and then our lambs at a price that covered both the costs of production and the costs of living very simply.

It was our experience of drovers and agents (who may well have a useful though limited role to play in some situations) and of auction barns and contracts, that led us to intervene on our own behalf in the marketplace, or, in the language of current ideology, to engage in 'trade-distorting measures'. In the process of organizing a shipment of lambs to an out-of-province buyer, I went to the weekly auction to buy lambs to fill the truck. I made more money off those lambs in one day as a dealer than I could make in a year as a farmer. Reporting on this at the annual meeting of the Sheep Producers Association made me a few enemies and led us into the work of establishing a farmer owned and operated cooperative to market all of our lambs. This opened the door to direct involvement in every aspect of the livestock industry and, indeed, of the food distribution business. As a co-operative, we sold lambs for almost every commercial producer in the province and dealt every day with the region's largest distributor/retailer. We also had to learn about dealing with government regulatory agencies and the business of butchering.

When we sold the farm and moved back to Toronto, we left behind the Northumberland Lamb Marketing Co-op and the Brookside Abattoir Co-op, which both continued to function as farmer owned and operated co-operatives. *Northumberlamb*, as it is known, is a non-share capital co-operative, meaning that the structure of the co-operative does not encourage the accumulation of equity or capital. The return to the owners, who are its members, is in the form of the service and price they receive as they utilize the co-op. Thus the refrigerated truck is owned not by the members, but by the co-op as a collective. When we quit farming, we could not endanger the co-op by withdrawing capital from it, since it was deliberately designed *not* to be a vehicle for capital accumulation.

Cathleen and I raised two children, probably the most important crop we grew, on that farm, and when the younger leapfrogged through school so that she was ready to leave home the same year her older brother was, we had to make some hard decisions.

Fifteen years is, in fact, about one generation on the farm. Usually the farm grows with the family, once the kids are on their feet (literally). When they are 16 or 18, and ready to either leave or take a greater role in the farm, it becomes necessary to make conscious decisions with every member of the family participating. Too often this does not happen, and the story often has an unhappy ending. In our case, it was obvious that our children should go on to university, but by that time we were so involved in organizing and political work that we had become quite dependent on their presence. If we were away at a meeting, or on co-op business, we could count on the kids to do the chores. We had also increased our land base and our flock with their help, and without them we would have to hire help. But the farm could not afford that. Like most farms, we had survived on the basis of the exploitation of family labour, however much we enjoyed it.

We opted for the organizing, the political work, and a new life. We didn't go broke, and because we ignored the advice of all the business advisors and agents, we managed to sell our farm piece by piece and come out of it with enough to move back to Toronto and carry on. In a sense that was the conclusion of a long chapter. When we left Toronto in 1971 we sold our house for what we thought was a good price. We bought the farm, complete with machinery and cattle, for one-third of what we had sold our house for. After 15 years of building up the farm, and reinvesting every penny we ever made, we sold the whole thing for about a quarter of the current price of our former Toronto house.

It all added up to a significant learning experience, the sort of experience one does not get in school or from books. It was the desire to share that experience and its teachings that produced the first edition of this book. Looking back now, a few more years down the road, I can also see the farm experience as a rather long and necessary apprenticeship to the understanding I now have of the food system, and the basis of my conviction that we have to grasp and invert its logic.

INTRODUCTION

Biting into a freshly picked tomato from a local sustainable system (your own garden, for example) bears little resemblance to the experience of eating a tomato chemically grown in Mexico or Florida with cheap labour and trucked the thousands of miles to northern markets in January.

Planting the best seed saved from last years crop in commonly held land fertilized with composted manure and other 'waste', and with it planting companion crops to maintain diversity and resist pests, is the beginning of a sustainable food system. It is not, however, the food system most of us experience, the system we must begin to comprehend if we are going to create just and sustainable food systems.

This book is not simply an itemized, piece-by-piece description of supermarkets and farms, nutrition and starvation, sharing and accumulation. It is a book about *how* the food system functions and how it might function. I refer to this as the *logic* of the food system because I am quite sure that it is possible for virtually anyone to grasp this logic, and in so doing to gain tools that can serve to liberate from the fatalism and sense of powerlessness that is so common in Western culture. The logic I refer to can be expressed in the concept of *distancing*: separating people from the sources of their food and nutrition with as many interventions as possible.

The development of this food system need not be ascribed to either ill will or benevolence, but it is, nevertheless, a global, integrated system organized to fulfil a single purpose: the accumulation of wealth. Just as it organizes accumulation, it must organize deprivation. With its only ethic that of growth, the Market Economy of food must continue to extend its frontiers and its logic. This leaves little room for diversity, sustainability, or regional economies. It also reinforces the ideology that there is only one way to organize an economy.

I use the term 'food system' to refer to a highly integrated system that includes everything from farm input suppliers to retail outlets, from farmers to consumers. I use it in the singular to reflect the domination of a single world-wide system, although there are still many local, though rapidly disappearing, food systems around the world. The globalization of production, processing and distribution in this system is reflected in the labels in a supermarket or can be experienced while walking through an ethnic neighbourhood in a large city: our food comes from everywhere in every conceivable form.

The integrated character of the food system, and the characteristics that make it a system, are not so obvious to the untrained eye. The appearance is one of great diversity and many participants, whether as retailers, processors, growers, or wholesalers. There are superstores and corner stores, specialty shops and franchised everythings. On the menu or on the shelf there are hundreds and thousands of choices. But can we make a meaningful 'choice' among 30,000 items?

In the countryside there are huge farms and little farms, bankrupt farms and 'successful' farms. It is often hard to tell the difference. Feed and machinery companies appear under many names, although their numbers are rapidly diminishing. There are also chemical and seed companies. One could easily believe that there are many different brands and companies competing in the marketplace.

But the agricultural chemicals, like the seeds and the machinery, will almost all come from one of four to six transnational corporations in each sector. (Four now seems to be the lowest number for sustainable oligopoly, but in the first edition of this book I said six!) The machinery will be an assemblage of globally sourced components sold under four different corporate names, none of them Canadian.[1] The buyers of agricultural commodities may seem legion to the outsider, but chances are that for any single farm product there are between one and four actual buyers, without accounting for possible collusion between the visible players.

Appearances notwithstanding, the food system is tightly integrated as a system. There may be many puppets, but there are few puppeteers. It is one thing to count up and describe all the pieces of a system, however, but something quite different to understand its *logic*: how it works and what its rules are, as well as who benefits and who loses. Examining carefully the structures and mechanisms, the logic, of power and control is something we are not often encouraged to do.

Food systems are cultural expressions. The North American food system is dominated by the culture of Science and Technology which would have us believe that the whole is nothing but the sum of its parts, and that each part, or building block, is a stable, well-defined object that interacts clearly with other objects through the forces of nature. This is *Reductionism*. Such a mechanistic view of reality assumes that once we know how individual building blocks behave, we can determine how a collection of building blocks will behave. It is this view that leads us to believe that a description of the products and the structures, the building blocks, of a food system will provide us with as much understanding of the food system as we can achieve, even though such an understanding leaves us powerless.

A food system, however, is not simply composed of a number of static or dead parts. Its components constantly interact with each other and with their environment. A food system, like an organism, can only be understood and described in terms of behaviour, that is, how the parts interact. To try to describe the food system in reductionist terms is like trying to describe the process of feeding a growing family by enumerating the contents of the cupboards and the cooking utensils. Such an exercise will describe some of the ingredients that make up a domestic food system, but it would hardly explain how the children are persuaded to eat their broccoli.

The logic of our food system owes much to the economic and scientific thinking and social organization of 17th and 18th-century England. Reductionist, linear science coupled with the abstractions of natural law and natural theology were reinforced by Victorian piety and individualism. "The survival of the fittest" as a creed suited well the purposes of those who sought to reduce society to the functioning of a global marketplace, and human community to a federation of classes, a continuing struggle of winners and losers.

The reduction of food to a commodity and the reduction of persons to consumers and customers are logical expressions of this 19th and now late 20th-century ideology. The unwillingness or inability to imagine or consider alternatives to reductionism is a reflection of the power of determinist science, or "the laws of nature". The passive acceptance by the religious community of the interpretation of God as the great clockmaker in the sky who created the universe, established the Natural Law and then retired, imbued reductionism with the credibility and power to establish its domination and banish all alternatives from consideration.

To move beyond this system of exploitation, we must understand the logic of *distancing* and then turn it inside-out. When we do this, we come up with the characteristics, or logic, of *Proximity, Diversity,* and *Balance.* These, and their 'expressions' like Community Shared Agriculture that have begun to take shape since the first edition of this book was written, are explored in the latter chapters of this book. These alternate principles have always been the basis of those food systems that have sustained Native communities, whether in the Arctic, in the mountains of Peru, the deserts of Africa, the rain forests of Central America or the coastlands of the world.

The central celebration of my own Christian faith, a celebration which has for long been marginalized as a purely cultic or spiritual exercise, may still inspire a vision of our possible life together. The Eucharist, or Communion, is a proclamation that there is enough for all if the economy is organized for indefinite sharing, not short-term accumulation. No human community can exist on any other basis. Violence and repression are otherwise required to keep the deprived from taking back what has been taken from them. Human communities are thus destroyed; but community, like food, is essential to life.

CHAPTER 1

THE LANGUAGE OF DISTANCING AND THE PROCESS OF COMMODIFICATION

> During the 15 years we farmed in Nova Scotia we grew forage crops and raised beef cattle, sheep, chickens, dogs, and two children. We regarded ourselves as farmers. We never thought of referring to ourselves as 'children producers'.

People do not normally submit to starvation just because no-one has been around marketing some product for them to consume. Eating is one of our most basic urges, and given an adequate income with which to purchase food, or the opportunity to produce it for themselves, people will see to it that they get enough to eat.

In North America, it was not too long ago that in the spring of the year farmers would prepare their land to receive the seeds that they had selected as the best, for their purposes, from their last year's crop. As the ground was warming, equipment was repaired and the winter's accumulation of manure spread on the land. The farmer did not have to go to the bank, or the local feed and chemical supplier, to arrange credit and to order the hybrid seed, the agro-toxins, and the fertilizer required for the planting season. And the farmer did not need to be a licensed mechanic or a computer buff to get started. The farmer's knowledge, and the secrets and the wisdom of the land being worked, were passed from generation to generation, as oral history that could be shared by every member of the community. Farmers planted, tended, and harvested *food*, for themselves and their households. It was stored and prepared at home, without the aid of shrink-wrap and Tetra Pak, cryovac or micro-wave. The left-overs probably went to the pig or the chickens, without need of a truck to haul away the packaging materials. The jars would be used again next year.

> I overheard the comment one day, "You can tell he's a farmer by the grease under his fingernails". What a strange identification for a steward of the land, a gardener or one who cares for livestock, I thought.

For food to become business it has first to be transformed, at least in our heads, into commodities, because a market economy functions by means of commodity exchange. This means that in our language and thinking we have to separate food from its function of providing nutrition, and turn it instead into a means of making money. Food becomes *product* that has value only in so far as it can be traded in and speculated on. It is logical that we then have to *market* the *product* because it no longer has any intrinsic value to people. "This little piggy goes to market" turns into, "This little product is marketed". And now I go to a folk concert and it is announced that there is 'product' – casettes and CD's – for sale at the kiosk to the left!

Referring to real live (or dead) pig as 'product' neutralizes it, replacing its use-value with its exchange-value. A pig is transformed by language from something alive that we butcher and eat to some *thing* that is marketed, an object with no intrinsic value and no longer any intrinsic relationship to life, or to hunger and human need.

Marketing itself is the process of creating a need that can be satisfied only through the purchase of the product being marketed. For example, fast-food industry executives describe their business as market-driven, with the differences between fast-food chains being established not through different products, but

through product differentiation achieved by advertising and public relations. McDonald's alone spends some $750-million per
year in global advertising, and its outlets in hospitals (20 of them
in U.S. hospitals by mid-1991) may be worth more as advertising
– the association established between McDonald's and health –
than as places to sell food.

Of course, in terms of nutrition, the process of feeding ourselves well is now severely distorted by costly and sophisticated
advertising and promotion, which colours our environment and
shapes our psyche from birth onwards about what is good, proper
and socially acceptable to eat and drink. In 1992, advertising ex-
penditures in all media by the food corporations or the food sectors of diversified corporations in Canada alone, totalled $365
million. This does not include in-store advertising, coupons and
other gimmicks, and various forms of display advertising, from
billboards to sports teams. To this one should add the other marketing charges such as slotting fees (fees charged to the distributor or manufacturer by powerful retailers as the entry fee for
getting shelf-space – a 'slot' – in the store).

In the rash of food industry takeovers in the 1980s (see
Chapter 3), it was often brand names, like Kraft, General Mills
and Nabisco – names on products that could be found in virtually
every store regardless of who owned the store – that were really
being bought. Investors attached more value to the names on the
product labels than the food they were applied to or than the
volume of business that could be done in generics (products labelled only 'onions' or 'flour' or 'bacon'). This attests to the role
of advertising and public identity in the food business.

In 1988, breakfast was the hot item, with Canadians spending $1.4
billion on 'breakfast products'. By 1993, breakfast cereals were an $8
billion market in North America, and Kellogg sold $60 million worth
of Corn Flakes and Frosted Flakes in Canada alone in 1992! The
major breakfast players and their market shares are:

Kellogg: 37.9%
General Mills: 25.0%
Post (Kraft General Foods): 14.4% (incl. Nabisco)
Quaker Oats: 6.9%
Ralston-Purina: 4.8%[2]

As language itself is used to transform food into an object of business – lamb becomes 'product' and corn becomes 'Corn Flakes' – so too is it used to transform farming into commodity production and to alienate a farmer from her or his own labour. For example, farmers frequently talk about 'profit' when what they really mean is wages, or 'a living'. Farmers have been taught by agricultural economists to use the word 'profit' for any surplus that remains from the sale of a crop after the cash costs (*excluding* the farmer's labour and any return on investment) have been paid. Of course this puts the farmer in a very strange position because the labour of the farmer and the farm family is then not considered a cost of production. This obviously misrepresents reality. In corporate accounting 'profit' is the surplus *after* all wages, salaries, directors fees, and costs have been paid.

In getting farmers and others to use the word 'profit' wrongly, agricultural economists and the ideologues of the Market Economy succeed in their task of convincing farmers and the public that the purpose of producing food is simply to make money, and that if there is anything left to live on after cash costs are paid their farm is 'profitable'. Of course farmers, along with everyone else, should make a decent living, but being paid fairly for the work one does is vastly different from defining what one does solely in terms of making money, or, in the case of farmers particularly, making a profit. Dairy farmers under supply-management marketing boards, as they still are in Canada, have a cost-of-production pricing formula which assures them of making a decent living – at least in theory – but not a profit. Farmers not under supply management, particularly in hogs or beef, are assured of nothing. Since what they receive for what they produce depends more on market conditions over which they have no control than any amount of good management or hard work they may do, they may receive a windfall profit or they may make nothing.

It took me about two years of actually farming to really comprehend that, to understand that I could have a cow bred in the summer, feed her all through the winter, watch her calf being born, raise it to 400-500 lbs. and sell it in the fall, and have virtually nothing to show for it. We learned something about 'value-added' and where the money was to be made when we slaughtered and cut up our beef animals and sold the meat in 25 lb. lots at the farmer's market. That got us through the year when accepting the prices for live cattle would have ruined us, but it was still an awful lot of work for small reward.

Market Economy theory and its propagandists also use the term 'competitive', meaning the willingness to sell a product for a price as low as, or lower than, any other seller of the same commodity or product, without regard to the conditions or relations of production. Thus, if Haiti is compelled to sell sugar, because it has debts to pay and nothing else to sell for foreign currency, to the Redpath (Tate and Lyle) refinery in Toronto for five or ten cents a pound, utilizing labour to produce it that is paid little or nothing, is that a competitive or an exploitative price? (Particularly when the cost of producing sugar from beets in Canada is about 20-25 cents per pound.) In retailing, one often sees prices advertised as 'competitive', meaning that they are either low, or close to prices in other stores in the area. It may be that 'cheap' is not used as much these days because it does not have the same moral character as 'competitive' in our individualistic culture.

To be non-competitive is to be immoral in the theology of the Market Economy, and the term 'competitive' is used to manipulate and distract, to keep us from asking why prices for primary products are too low to provide an adequate return to their producers, wherever they might be. This gap between the costs of production and the price paid to the farmer is the major cause of the current crisis in the rural economy of North America which is commonly called the farm crisis. Identifying the problem as a 'farm crisis' makes it possible for urban residents to remain unaware of the wider social consequences of the exodus of farmers from the land, the consolidation of farms, and the destruction of rural communities. The same process occurs in the Third World. For the World Bank, the IMF, and transnational capital, the words of choice for this distortion, wherever it is found, are 'structural adjustment' and 'rationalization'.

A stunning example of the use of language to commodify food and everything else is the following, which transforms labour, including the work of management, from a human activity into 'human capital':

On economic grounds, justification for government intervention to mitigate adjustment costs is limited. The neo-classical
assumption is that gains from adjustment exceed the costs;
therefore, intervention is only justified in the event of market
failure. One market that may have imperfections is that for
human capital.[3]

Similarly, a newspaper article analysing the 1988 agricultural census reported that "the census shows that 66% of farm
women work . . . The women have a variety of occupations". The
reporter is not talking about women working on the farm, as they
always have, but about women taking off-farm employment. This
reflects the same acceptance of commodification: if you do not
have a wage or salaried job, you are not working. Work is not
defined by what is done, but by its exchange value. Applied to the
vast numbers of people, from peasant farmers in the Third World
to urban women who raise children and farm kids who do adult
work after school, whose labour is either essentially outside a
money economy or simply unpaid, it defines a large portion of the
world's productive labour as *not work*.

The 1991 Canadian farm census did reflect some change in
thinking, identifying the number of women farmers, but the substantial increase in numbers from the 1986 census went unex-
plained. Was it simply that the farm wives were actually counted
this time as farmers, or were there more women farming on their
own? To understand the social context, and break out of the fatalism fostered by the deliberate (mis)use of language, one must
first objectify or de-mystify the language.

Once farmers and their advisors, suppliers, or buyers have
come to regard food as a commodity, or simply a raw material for
further processing, then it is easy to apply criteria such as uniformity, durability, and herbicide resistance to the character and
production of that commodity. Criteria such as nutritional value,
flavour, and natural disease resistance become quite secondary, if
not irrelevant.

In selecting a good breeding line for fresh market tomatoes,
breeders have always looked at yield, fruit size, lack of defects,
and disease resistance. All those characteristics are vitally important, but so is taste.[4]

Once food has become only a commodity or a raw material, the notion of adding *value* also becomes reasonable. If the point is to make as much money out of the commodity as possible before it is finally consumed or thrown out, then it also becomes reasonable to process, transform, and transport the product as much as possible in order to maximize the spread – the profit opportunities – between the cost of the raw material and the final product on the grocery store shelf.

The less real nutrition in any given product, the more room for profit. Protein is expensive, relative to bulk. The lamb that was compact and firm always weighed more than the rangy soft lamb, just as the protein value of the feed could be judged by its weight for bulk. A bale of low-protein hay will weigh considerably less than a bale of green alfalfa hay of the same size.

If more wheat can be sold at a lower price if it contains less protein, that is what 'the market' (the traders and processors, who work on commission or margin) will demand. High protein bread as a quality food is *not* the goal. As for vitamins, it is cheaper to add synthetic vitamins later. Cargill Ltd. has been pushing for a number of years now to get Canadian farmers to give up growing high-protein hard red spring wheat in favour of cheaper, mid-quality wheat because the same acreage would produce a greater volume of grain, and Cargill trades in volume, not nutrition: "Our challenge is to grow more tons, value add to more meat, value add again to more further processing."[5]

> While ground mustard seed has been used in food systems for thousands of years, its use has been limited by the uncontrollable 'mouth-heat' it develops. Now a food scientist has developed a way to 'de-heat' mustard seed. Since consumers are concerned about chemical additives in food, it is advantageous to be able to list deheated ground mustard seed on the package as a 'spice', although its function is to replace stabilizers and preservatives. "Because of its high protein content (30-40%) deheated ground mustard seed can be used to reduce some of the meat content, thus reducing costs. . ."[6]

McDonald's is in the business of selling french fries, not nutrition, so they want product (potatoes) that cook to their specifications, not healthy potatoes with high protein content that provide a high level of nutrition without chemical residues. But it is the consumer who gets blamed for demands and specifications which are actually made by the profit-takers in the food system.

Another step in this process of commodification and the reduction of food to raw materials is its further reduction to a 'feedstock'. This refers not to cattle feed, but to the grain or milk or whatever when it is treated as a raw material for an industrial process that utilizes only certain of its components. In this case, the raw material – what might otherwise be called food – is broken down by one process or another into its constituent parts so that they can then be recombined, or combined with other substances, to form a new desert or a drink, a cereal or a garbage bag. Thus corn can be reduced to proteins and enzymes and starches to become an ingredient in a host of products, which may or may not be edible (like gasoline). Through ultrafiltration, milk can be similarly reduced to a collection of components which can be recombined into whatever product will maximize profit.

A liquid diet for persons who cannot digest solids will be launched by Nestlé Enterprises Ltd. with the help of a federal repayable contribution of $1,001,300. The diet can be ingested orally or by naso-gastric tube and will be made from Canadian raw materials.[7]

Four new products have been added to the Dairyland Products line. Melopro 7500 and Melopro 7600 are isolated wheat protein products that have excellent functional characteristics and perform well as partial or total casein replacers . . . recommended for use in breading batters, diet beverages, meat analogue, and breakfast cereals.[8]

In February, 1990, U.S. Government regulators approved the first use of a fat substitute called Simplese in frozen desserts. Simplese is made by cooking and blending egg white and milk protein. Wall Street analysts said the new product could be worth up to $300 million a year to its manufacturer, Monsanto Co.'s subsidiary NutraSweet.[9] A year later NutraSweet announced a new form of Simplese based on whey protein concentrate rather than milk protein that could be used in a wide variety of foods and projected a $16 billion market for its fat replacers.[10]

This is only one aspect of the *deconstruction* of food. The reduction of food to a product, commodity, raw material, or feedstock is taken at least one step further. This step we could describe as the *vaporization* of food, and it occurs when food is transformed into a speculative commodity that can be traded on the futures market. It is 'futures' trading because it is trading in a commodity that will only physically exist at some time in the future. Neither the buyer nor the seller can actually touch or own the commodity they are trading because it has yet to be grown or harvested. (Technically the seed may have actually been planted, but the crop does not yet exist.)

There is, of course, a past along with the 'futures'. Before food could be commodified, as William Cronon describes in his fascinating history of Chicago, the land itself had to be commodified: "Fields, fences, and firebreaks were concrete embodiments of the environmental partitioning that made farming possible, but they also expressed the underlying property system that divided the land into ownership rights." The implement for this process was "A vast grid of square-mile sections whose purpose was to turn land into real estate. . . By imposing the same abstract and homogeneous grid pattern on all land, no matter how ecologically diverse, government surveyors made it marketable."[11]

The commodification of land certainly made it easier to commodify what the land produced, and grain elevators and grading systems helped this transformation of grain by making it tradable in large quantities regardless of where it had come from. That is, the food became detached and distanced from the land that yielded it. It was then but a short step into the futures market, where the grain that was traded had no physical existence at all.

> Wheat and grain came to Chicago from farms that were themselves radical simplifications of the grassland ecosystem. . . An older grain-marketing system had preserved the fine distinctions among these natural and human diversities by maintaining the legal connection between physical grain and its owner.[12]

Once the metaphysics of commodification of the land and then the crop that grew upon it had become "second nature", it was, seemingly, only logical to take the process one step further, that is, to make the right to trade in futures itself a commodity: in 1875 the Chicago Board of Trade decided that its own memberships "should also be offered for sale in the open market as commodities in their own right."[13]

The line between futures trading and metaphysics is much finer than the line between growing food to eat and buying a contract for pork bellies for next July, but now even the paper on which the contract was once recorded is disappearing, like the crop itself, to be replaced by electronic information that one cannot lay hands on.

When an Australian transnational, Elders IXL Ltd., decided to become a big-league player in the grain business in the late 1980s, its corporate promotional material described its view of global grain trading:

> Electronic trading of rural produce is developing dramatically .
> . . With the specifications now used to describe precise qualities
> of grain, enquiring about, negotiating and closing the deal will
> soon be possible through electronic screens.

So food, as if by magic, undergoes transformations into 'rural produce', a raw material, a commodity, or a contract. At the last stage of this profit-production process is the consumer, not as a person, but as a function of the system, making room for more product to be produced and more profit to accrue. For its part, Elders went as fast as it had come, sent packing by the established grain industry in a quiet display of their oligopolistic control of the trade. ('Oligopoly' refers to a cosy relationship among a few large firms for purposes of protecting and enhancing their collective welfare.)

Farmers, like their crops, are also transformed: first into consumers of agricultural inputs, then into producers, and finally into *businessmen*. Farmers are indoctrinated to use this last word in reference to themselves. Obviously the word is sexist; beyond that, the primary work of the farmer is not to do business but to grow food and raise livestock. The farmers who unwittingly allow the use of this term, and use it in reference to themselves, are apt to become alienated from their own work or vocation and become instead objects in a system controlled by others. ('Businessman' serves the same purpose as 'profit'.) The term 'half-ton farmer' is used in some places to describe the farmer who spends most of his time running around in his pick-up truck 'doing business', that is, buying, selling and making deals.

More recently, even the word 'farm' has become unacceptable. It is increasingly rendered as 'farm business' – yet another step in the distancing of the farmer from farming and the transformation of the entire farm operation into a commodity system.

Product, then, is produced by a businessman running a farm business. The raw material is processed and finally marketed through an outlet (like a field drain emptying into a ditch that carries the water away) to a consumer. Statistics Canada accounts for this process as the 'disappearance' of commodities or food. Given the impossibility of accounting for food in terms of how much is spoiled, eaten, fed to animals, removed in processing, put in the garbage, etc., it is a reasonable accounting procedure, but the irony should not be lost. Like pig (or pork) being turned into product, persons are turned into consumers, and consumers are only valued if they have the money to become customers. The value of consumers is directly related to their function as a means of getting rid of product, like a Dispose-All, garbage can, or just another length of tubing in the cosmic plumbing system!

The person who cannot become a consumer because he/she does not have the money to be a customer faces the alternatives of welfare or food banks. It then becomes the responsibility of those who do have money to pay their taxes *and* either donate money to charity or become surrogate customers on behalf of the deprived. Major food distributors like George Weston Ltd. (Loblaws) are high-profile supporters of food banks and food drives. It helps their public image, it helps to keep the product moving, and it helps their balance-sheet if the middle class can be persuaded to become sponsors for the deprived by *buying* processed foods and then, on the far side of the check-out, donating them to the food banks. On the other hand, this process also diverts the energy that should be pressing for an increase in welfare benefits to tide people over while a food system devoted to feeding people is created.

The reduction of people to functions is an essential premise of a capitalist economy, in the same way that information has to be reduced to a zero-based code to be processed by a computer, whether on the futures market or at the check-out. Otherwise biological and social considerations such as malnutrition and starvation would introduce 'irrational' factors into the system.

We are well along the way of completely separating – *distancing* – human nutrition from the growing of food, interposing vast and expensive industrial processes between human beings and the very simple basis of their existence.

CHAPTER 2

THE BIBLICAL ECONOMY OF FOOD

In striking contrast to the transformation of food that we have been describing are the stories and visions about food in the Biblical tradition. In the Hebrew scriptures and the New Testament, and thus for Jews and Christians, food occupies a central place both in the expression of faith and in social organization. My own critique of our current food system, and my vision of other systems, is informed by these stories and their statements about faith and its social consequences.

Christianity offers a powerful and potentially liberating paradigm (model) for a food system, and, perhaps, for an entire economy, in the Eucharist. The celebration of the Last Supper of Jesus has always been the central liturgical *act* of the Christian faith, however distorted and hidden it may have become at times.

The Eucharist is the church's celebration of the Feast of the Passover, which Jesus ate with his chosen community: the community that he gathered about him and invested much energy in building. As Jesus shared the Passover meal, the Jewish celebration of liberation from slavery, he turned it into his last official supper with his disciples, a feast that marked the beginning of the end for him. But if it was the beginning of the end, Jesus also recognized the dimension of promise in the words of the Passover service, "Next year in Jerusalem". His followers would not share the Passover again with him, but they would participate in the feast that would mark the beginning of the Reign of God, a new era, and the renewing of Creation.

The celebration of a key event in the history of the Jewish people took on a present meaning: the celebration of community and shared life, and with it, death. But it also took on the character of promise, becoming a paradigm of hope. The followers of Jesus were to look forward to the transformation of the world. The last would be first, the hungry would have enough to eat, and the mighty would be brought low.

The Eucharist – as act and promise – states unequivocally that God provides enough for all, and all of God's creatures are to share the sustenance of life equitably.

The Passover, however, was only the beginning. After the Jews escaped from bondage in Egypt they got delayed in the wilderness for "40 years" enroute to the promised land. They began to panic and complain and to rebel against God as well as against their leader Moses, telling themselves that the slavery of Egypt was to be preferred to the uncertainty, barrenness, and hardship of wilderness, because at least in Egypt they had all they could eat. The Exodus story then tells of how God provided Manna for them, so that they would know that "I, Yahweh, am your God".

> . . . in the morning there was a coating of dew all around the camp. When the coating of dew lifted, there on the surface of the desert was a thing delicate, powdery, as fine as hoarfrost on the ground. When they saw this, the children of Israel said to one another, What is that? not knowing what it was. "That", said Moses to them, "is the bread Yahweh gives you to eat. This is Yahweh's command: everyone must gather enough of it for their needs, one omer a head, according to the number of persons in your families. Each of you will gather for those who share your tent."
>
> The children of Israel did this. They gathered it, some more, some less. When they measured in an omer what they had gathered, the one who had gathered more had not too much, the one who had gathered less had not too little. Each found they had gathered what they needed.
>
> Moses said to them, "No one must keep any of it for tomorrow". But some would not listen and kept part of it for the following day, and it bred maggots and smelt foul; and Moses was angry with them. Morning by morning they gathered it,

each according to their needs. And when the sun grew hot, it melted.[14]

The story does not end there. On the sixth day they gathered twice as much, and when they reported this to Moses, Moses told them that it was all right, that God wanted the seventh day to be a day of complete rest, a Sabbath. They were to eat half of what they gathered on the sixth day and the other half on the Sabbath. To their surprise, the Manna did not rot that time, and there was enough for the Sabbath, but no more.

This story is the paradigm of a just and equitable food system, a system in which distancing is excluded by the structure of the system itself. The very character of the Manna precluded the possibility of speculation. Those entrepreneurs who thought they would gather some extra that they might sell the next day to the shiftless who had not gathered enough got a surprise. Manna, not being a commodity, could not be hoarded or bought and sold for a profit. Even the Sabbath arrangement left no room for merchants. As food, the Manna spoiled the minute some opportunist thought it could be turned into a commodity in which one could profiteer or speculate. Food, faith, and justice were inextricably bound together.

In the Eucharist, which means literally 'thanksgiving', there is always enough bread and wine for everyone present. It would be an unthinkable abomination for the presiding officer to announce part-way through the feast: "Sorry, no more today. Come back next Sunday and we may be able to feed you." Nor is there a charge for either the sustenance or the service, though there are records of such attempts being made.

The Eucharist is a communal act and an act of community, not a matter of life insurance. It is a feast in which all participate, receiving food and drink for the body and the spirit from the hands of their brothers and sisters, in solidarity with those who have gone before, those yet to come, and with all who inhabit God's Creation now.

Unlike life insurance, or magic rituals with which individuals may try to insulate themselves from the uncertainties of both life and human community or interdependence, the Eucharist proclaims that security lies in reliance not on one's own savings and shrewdness, but in mutual dependence within a contemporary community.

The Eucharist, as a paradigm of the banquet in the new Creation, is a proclamation of how God invites us to live in and with Creation and to organize the economy of our household.

CHAPTER 3

DISTANCING: THE LOGIC OF THE FOOD SYSTEM

FROM LAND TO MOUTH

I have already used the term *distancing* in hinting at the processes that are separating people from the sources of their food and replacing diversified and sustainable food systems with a global commodified food system. This chapter explores the variety of interventions which increase the distance between land and mouth.

Distancing most obviously means increasing the physical distance between the point at which food is actually grown or raised and the point at which it is consumed, as well as the extent to which the finished product is removed from its raw state by processing.

There was a time when food was grown within the daily experience of just about everybody. Almost every woman was involved in its production and processing (as in much of Third World and wherever sustenance agriculture is practised today), and it was consumed, more or less, on the spot. To a great extent there was no choice because there was virtually no way to transport food and no means of preserving it in a form that could be transported, beyond drying or salting.

The relatively recent invention of the steam engine, the internal combustion engine, and refrigeration initiated the industrialization of agriculture. (The first boat-load of refrigerated meat arrived in England from Australia in 1879, according to one account, while another source reports that it was United Fruit in 1903 that began the successful refrigeration of fruit shipped by sea.)

Vegetables and fruit could not be hauled thousands of miles overland without both modern refrigeration and modern trucking. The latest stage of this development is, of course, jet aircraft which, because of their speed, have reduced the need for refrigeration, while adding to the costs and making it possible for wealthy markets to be supplied with food grown virtually anywhere in the world. Jet-set tomatoes can be grown in the irrigated desert of Israel and flown to the Toronto market the next day. Cargill Inc., noted for its movement of bulk commodities by water, has developed a special process and special bulk tanker ships to haul frozen orange juice concentrate from Brazil to New Jersey and Rotterdam where it is packaged. The trip takes five days. For a price, both seasonality and locality can be eliminated.

Biotechnology is just the latest application of this same principle of distancing. The intentional modification of genetic material, in plants and animals, requires time and money, and the commercialization of research can be very disappointing. But when it is successful, it radically alters traditional relationships between farmers and their seeds, creating both economic dependencies – for seeds, fertilizers and agro-toxins – and altered social relations.[15] Control over the direction and management of the food system continues to pass from those who grow and eat the food into the hands of fewer and fewer people in fewer and fewer corporate boardrooms, vastly increasing the distance between the crop and both the farmer and the consumer.[16]

Another way to view this is by looking at the production of wheat on the prairies. Without the steam-powered threshing machine, the railroad, and then the combine, industrialized wheat monoculture was out of the question, to say nothing of the scale of present grain production. Quite apart from anything else, the population of the prairies could never consume anything like all the wheat grown there. Without modern transportation and food preservation techniques, agriculture could only remain at a subsistent or self-reliant level. Without technology, distance is hardly an issue, and every technological intervention increases distance. The more perishable a commodity is, the more this is true.

The separation of raw food production from the consumers of the final product happens in many ways. The effect of all of them is to increase the distance in the food system:

□ by breeding and engineering stability, durability and 'shelf-life' into a commodity;

□ by physically increasing the distance between where food is grown and where it is consumed;

□ by processing and product differentiation which increases the distance between the raw food and the end-product;

□ by adding preservation techniques and substances so that the time between when the food was alive and when it is consumed is increased;

□ by packaging technologies that permit longer storage and greater handling and shipping;

□ by urbanizing a population so that it no longer has a rural or farm experience, regardless of physical distance from the land. (For example, in 1951 only 57% of the Canadian population lived in urban (10,000 or more) areas and by 1981 this had increased to 76%. 1991 figures cannot be directly compared due to a change in the definition of 'urban', but it would appear the trend has slowed while many rural areas have become more suburban.)

In any or all of these ways, people are alienated, or distanced, from the sources of their nutrition. Each act of distancing also introduces an opportunity for extracting money from the system and gaining control over it. The public may ostensibly pay less for their food, but at the same time the farmers, the primary producers get less for their 'product'. The emphasis shifts to what is now called 'value added', meaning any and all interventions which add cost (and profit) to the final product. The result is that both food and nutrition are devalued while the economic activity in between is increasingly valued, and with 'value' in this sense goes control.

Historically, from hunter-gatherers and nomadic tribes to paddy-rice and subsistence farmers, the procurement, preparation and enjoyment of food has been a central cultural activity of human communities. In the industrialized world, however, it is hard to have any sense at all of where our food comes from, how it gets to us, or what happens to it along the way. Rather than being a focal point of our culture, food has become for us a business activity in which we participate as workers, customers, or consumers – and, one must add, owners and corporate shareholders. The experience of having a dinner party in a restaurant may still be an aspect of our culture, but it bears little resemblance to the rural wedding party where practically everything is locally grown and prepared at home. Perhaps this is why immigrant ethnic communities 'bring their own' food – if not with them, then shortly afterwards, as they set up shop and either grow or import their cultural staples.

The attempt to provision oneself with familiar staple foods and condiments, whether produced locally or imported from the homeland, is a vastly different proposition from the deliberate production of commodity-food for export: the Pakistani community in Toronto importing their flavourful rice from home does not require that the local economy back home focus solely on growing that rice for export.

Much of the current economic, social and ecological distress that is being visited upon rural areas worldwide is the result of making commodity export the driving force of the economy. Production of food for export, as anything more than a residual activity, is the production of distancing. It creates space to be exploited by those in the middle, from exporters at one end to retailers at the other, and including the manufacturers of farm 'inputs' like hybrid seeds and agro-toxins.

Until very recently, there were few voices to be heard suggesting that the distancing resulting from the 'modernization' of food production, processing, and transportation was not *Progress*. Now, however, as the costs of this Progress become evident on farms and in rural communities around the world, and as this Progress destroys the environment and rural communities and produces hunger in North and South, there is an increasing willingness to question the entire system.

DISTANCING IN THE DAIRY INDUSTRY

Modern dairy farms illustrate the development of distancing very well. Before the present technology of dairy farming and milk production, dairy farms and dairies were small and located very close to the consuming population. Just forty years ago, fresh milk was still delivered by horse and wagon, as well as by truck, from the farm to a nearby dairy in cans, without refrigeration. The cans were of a size that could be manually handled, and they were not replaced by refrigerated holding tanks on farms (referred to as bulk tanks) until the 1960s. Cows were milked by hand into a bucket until electrification permitted the introduction of the vacuum pump, which was followed in the 1960s by the pipeline milker which could convey the milk from the milking machine directly to the bulk tank without being handled. The milking parlour, which houses all the milking equipment and through which the cows pass to be milked twice (or more) a day, is the latest mechanical/technological development, though many farmers continue to use a pipeline milker in conjunction with tie-stalls for their cows.

But milk tanks required milk tankers: trucks with stainless-steel tanks to haul the milk to the dairy for processing. The introduction of tank-trucks, however, also meant that the distance from the farm to the dairy could be increased since trucks could haul faster and further than horses. Then farmers had to improve their laneways to facilitate the use of trucks, and as the trucks have hauled further and gotten larger the laneways have probably had to be upgraded more than once, thereby influencing the location and layout of new dairy barns and even the abandonment of old ones that were inaccessible to bigger trucks.

Farm mechanization has been accompanied by a consistent trend toward bigger farms and fewer farms. It is generally assumed that this is the inevitable result of Progress; in my view it is neither inevitable nor good. Dairy farms have probably resisted this trend more than other types of farms, at least in Canada, but their numbers have declined and their production and size increased over the years. As farms have become fewer and farther between, cooperation of any kind has become more difficult. (See Chapter 7.)

As the literal distance between the source of milk on the farm and the consumer in the city has increased – the farms being driven by urbanization and the cost of land further and further from the urban centres – a tug-of-war of sorts has developed, at least in Canada, between the Milk Marketing Boards and the processors. Since the Milk Marketing Boards are responsible for getting the raw milk from the farm to the processor, they would like the processors to be located as close to the cows as possible, in order to reduce the transport costs incurred by the Boards and, in turn, by the farmers. The processors want just the reverse, preferring to keep their delivery costs as low as possible by locating the processing plants as close to the urban centres as possible. Nowhere is this more visible than in the case of Ault Foods' fluid milk plant, the largest one in Canada, located where its five big white raw milk silos are visible to everyone travelling on the Don Valley Parkway in and out of Toronto. ('AULT' on the silos is probably worth more in advertising than the $3.4 million Ault spent on advertising in 1992.)

On the consumer side of the dairy, it was common for milk to be delivered daily in glass bottles, unrefrigerated, to the door until the mid-60s. This kept the practical distance between dairy and customer to a minimum, and the traditional intimate relationship to milk as the prime nurturing food was maintained (as in the bedtime glass of warm milk). The disappearance of home delivery, was, in part, brought about by homogenization (literally shaking the whole milk until the fat molecules will no longer voluntarily separate as cream), which results in faster souring, and the universal application of refrigeration: after processing, during transport, and in the home. Now milk is advertised, successfully, as "Cold, Beautiful Milk!"

Refrigeration was only one of the technological innovations that permitted greater distancing of the consumer from the dairy and from the dairy farm. Sterilization (pasteurization) procedures, and just plain cleanliness, from cow to table, account for a lot of the development in this direction, and have contributed significantly to public health. As usual, however, there are other factors to consider, one of them being the growing recognition of 'lactose maldigestion', which many people attribute precisely to the efforts to sanitize and homogenize milk. While dieticians and doctors may claim that lactose maldigestion is genetic or ethnic, there are many other people who argue that at least some of it is the result of the changes produced in the whole milk solids (fats and proteins) in the process of pasteurization and homogenization. These people are more apt to believe their own experience than the scientism of the medical profession.

At the same time, the increasing ingestion of ultra-clean or sterile food probably contributes to the susceptibility of urban people in particular to a host of what are now hostile 'bugs', bugs to which they were once immune. This may not seem like a significant issue, but when one remembers that the gut is, in fact, a fermenting chamber, dependent for its functioning on a vast army of living micro-organisms permanently resident therein, it is only common sense that the ingestion of dead or sterile food is adding a significant burden to the digestive process, something like trying to start your car in Winnipeg in January without a block heater!

The little coffee creamers and the unrefrigerated milk-based drinks in cardboard cartons are other examples of new technologies which distance in the same way. They have been made possible by the development of a process called UHT (ultra-high-temperature) pasteurization. (Note the 'UHT' or 'Ultra-pasteurized' or 'Long-Life' on the creamer top.) This treatment of the milk to sterilize it is combined with aseptic (sterile) packaging, one of the more exciting and significant new technologies in the food system. Tetra Pak is the leading example of this packaging technology. The achievement of these combined technologies is that milk or other dairy products, as well as juices of all sorts, can be kept unrefrigerated for weeks without spoiling, thus facilitating longer and cheaper storage and transport, though it still amazes me to see coconut milk from Thailand in such containers in Toronto, or mango juice from China.

The UHT and aseptic packaging equipment for this process is very expensive and requires a high degree of utilization to rationalize the cost. Of course it also adds to the cost of the product, as does every intervention. The manufacturer of the packaging equipment, the processor who leases it, the corporation that transports it, etc., all have to be paid and they all expect to profit.

Initially there was just one UHT plant in Quebec, and it was capable of handling all the UHT requirements for the entire country. Some of the processors hoped to convince the rest that they should all utilize the one plant to treat the milk that they marketed in the 'difficult' (inaccessible) areas of the country where a longer shelf-life was really desirable. It was suggested that each processor could use their own label, and by all using the same plant they could spread the cost of this very expensive technology over the maximum amount of product. This genuine economic rationality did not win out, however, and now all but one of the provinces have under-utilized UHT plants. (There is a contradiction in this, I recognize. Having only one UHT plant would centralize production; on the other hand, centralized processing would have limited the drive to extend the use of the technology.) The cost of this irrationality is also, of course, passed along to the consumer.

The dairy processors, to rationalize their investments, also market orange and other juices that utilize the same processing and packaging technology. That is how the dairies got into the juice business, where they now have about half the market.

The process of distancing occurs everywhere. Indian activist and author Vandana Shiva told me that in her own country,

> the same thing is happening, where distribution is getting hooked up to production and you are distributing over longer distances, and if you distribute over longer distances you must process increasingly. Since you can't transport fresh milk over great distances, you turn it into cheese, but there aren't too many people who can afford to buy cheese. You say you have introduced a new commodity but what you don't say to the people is that in putting milk through processing plants (imported from the West), transporting it over long distances, and producing cheese for the elite, you have deprived the rural person of what milk (nutritional) base there was.
>
> Interestingly, the milk base in the rural areas was there for the poorest person because the way milk was preserved in India was not as milk, but as ghee, or butterfat, which was made out of curd. The buttermilk from the curd was always distributed to the poorest people of the village, it was always available free outside the house of the landlord, so you still had

a basic nutrient. The fat was taken away, but all the protein was in that buttermilk. With the making of cheese, buttermilk suddenly disappeared from the scene.[17]

INFANT FORMULA

As I began to revise this book, I was utterly amazed to realize how little I had said about breastfeeding and the infant formula business in the first edition. Obviously the manufacturing and marketing of infant formula, and consequently bottle-feeding, is the archetypal expression of distancing. There can be few acts more complex and more intimate than a woman breastfeeding a baby. There is certainly no more powerful example of the ideal food system – which may explain why the corporate sector has tried so hard to destroy this model and this experience by convincing, or forcing, every mother to bottle feed. The other reason, of course, is that infant formula is an immensely profitable business. It would not be nearly so profitable if it were limited to only those few mothers (such as adoptive parents) who really need to bottle-feed.

It is not unreasonable, in fact, to suggest that inserting a bottle between breast and baby is the primordial and most violent form that distancing takes in the food system. Yet because they play on the desires of the mother to provide the best possible care for her baby at a point at which she is highly vulnerable, the formula pushers are able to both assure the mother and subvert nature at the same time.

In a commodified culture, why should a woman not feel that she is incapable of feeding her infant adequately, since commodified food is superior in every respect, besides being modern and upper class. To think that you do not need the help of Nestlé or Wyeth or Ross Laboratories, with all their high-priced technology and expertise, is to be backward, to reject technology.

Mother and infant are both victims, but it is the infant who bears the greatest cost in consequent health problems, emotional deprivation, and, in much of the exploited world, mortality. It is not too harsh to describe the corporations that carry out this violent ($4 billion-a-year) conspiracy as murderers. (INFACT Canada says 3000-4000 babies a day die because they were not breastfed.)

FOOD IRRADIATION

A technology that is still struggling to makes its way in the market, and which has eaten up hundreds of millions of public dollars in research and development, is gamma irradiation of food. Marketed by the nuclear industry as a sanitizing and preservation technique that is utterly harmless, (though they still have no idea of what to do with the radioactive garbage), irradiation remains a stunning example of a technology in search of a market. Neither our food, nor anybody else's, needs it, but the nuclear industry desperately needs business. Like UHT processing, the irradiation of food introduces another cost factor and facilitates greater distancing in the food system. The promoters of the process claim that irradiated food is completely safe and can be stored for long periods of time without deterioration. They claim that this will be a boon to developing countries that need 'improved' food storage capability and are under pressure to produce cash crops for export in order to buy food and pay their debts. They neglect to say that the process is very expensive and will further increase the dependency of poor countries on export production in order to repay the loans required to buy a reactor. In addition food will have to be transported from where it is grown to the location of the irradiator which, because of its cost, will have to serve a very large growing area. For this reason it is likely to have only a negative impact on local nutrition.

A case in point is the irradiation facility installed in Thailand as an 'aid' project financed by the Canadian International Development Agency so that Thailand can grow and export more pineapples. This will cause peasant farmers to stop growing their own food and become wage labourers for a corporation like Del Monte or Dole. Atomic Energy Canada Ltd. (AECL) has been using this project for its own propaganda, claiming that this technology is wanted and needed by developing countries. (In 1988 the irradiation technology division of AECL changed its name to Nordion, a clear move to obscure the origins of the company and its business interests for the sake of public relations. 'Nordion' sounds so clean!)

Closer to home, in Mulberry, Florida, is Vindicator Inc. (an interesting choice of name), the first commercial food irradiation facility in North America. It started irradiating Florida strawberries for the North American market in January 1992, followed by onions, mushrooms and other fruit. New U.S. Food and Drug Administration regulations allow irradiated foods to be labelled as 'fresh', though they must be identified with the *radura* symbol. It's up to the consumer to recognize the significance of the little flower-like emblem.

New technologies are continually being developed that serve to increase the distance and corporate concentration in the food system, though they are always described as means of providing higher quality and more variety.

PROCESSING AND HEALTHY FOOD

Distancing in the food system means a decline in the real nutritive value of the food as well as an increase in its cost. A freshly picked tomato from the home garden is not the same thing as the one designed and 'developed' – or genetically engineered – for mechanical harvesting and days and thousands of miles of transportation. Anything picked fresh, and virtually still alive when eaten, is going to be of different nutritive value than something that has been dead or dying for days, refrigerated, and/or gassed into or out of a coma before it gets to you.

There are many stories of potato farmers refusing to eat the potatoes that they are growing for processing, and eating instead potatoes grown by their neighbours with minimal chemicals on healthier land. The potatoes that McCain's or Carnation (Nestlé) wants for processing into frozen french fries are inferior in many respects, not least nutritionally, because they are bred to have certain processing qualities and grown according to certain rules laid down by the processor. Besides the low protein content, such potatoes may not be well suited to the land on which they are grown and may be susceptible to diseases that other varieties are not, requiring higher usage of 'crop protection agents', i.e., agrotoxins. They may also be more difficult to store, requiring either costly facilities or high cullage. This is all on top of the problems created by single variety monoculture.

But virtually no commodity on the market today avoids a

compromise between the demands of the processor and the quality of the product. For example, when the solids content of a typical tomato is about 5% and the rest is water, with each 1% increase in the solids content saving processors $80-million a year through reduced transport and processing costs, will it be the consumer or the processor that determines the characteristics of the tomato?

The result is a high cost for the final product, but that does not mean the producer necessarily receives a higher price. The higher cost of the product is paid by the land in terms of deteriorating quality; by the producer in terms of deteriorating health due to exposure to a wide variety of toxins, and in terms of the cost of specialized equipment; and by the consumer who pays for the processing, the transportation, and the spoilage. The consumer also then gets what should be termed an inferior product, very often preserved, coloured and presented with the help of one or many additives. This includes watering the 'veggies' in the display case, not to keep them fresh, but to keep them appearing crisp – at the expense of the nutrients. The more dormant a vegetable or fruit is after picking, which means some degree of withering, the better it retains its nutritional value. Watering causes the vegetable to breathe and thus deteriorate, though it also does make the food appear fresher, as fresh as the morning dew!

Coming on the market in 1993, its manufacturer hopes, is a genetically engineered tomato which can be left to ripen on the vine and still have a three week shelf-life. Calgene, of Davis, California, in partnership with Campbell Soup Co., has found a way to reverse the 'aging' gene of the tomato and then clone the engineered plants. When they began their promotion in 1988, Robert Goodman of Calgene pointed out that, "Many advances have been made over the years in the genetics of the tomato by traditional plant breeding to allow it to be turned into an industrial crop . . ." He then described how 30% of the tomato crop grown on 150,000 acres in the central valley of California is not appropriate for harvesting at the optimal picking time because the tomatoes are either green or rotted and are consequently left in the field.

Calgene came to Campbell's assistance in the search for ways to achieve control of fruit ripening, so that all of the crop would be ready to harvest at the same time, through genetic engineering. Calgene scientists discovered that they could engineer a plant with the polygalacturonase gene turned around backwards, with the result that the phenotype of the plant is actually changed. The result was a tomato, they claim, that can be left on the vine to actually ripen and still have something like a ten-day shelf life before it turns to mush. The verdict on its eating quality is still out, and may be for some time as such genetically engineered foods arouse regulatory concern and public resistance.

The first field trial of these new plants took place in Mexico in 1988 because the company had not received permission to conduct such tests in the United States. The concern was with the potential consequences of novel organisms proliferating in the environment with results we cannot possibly foresee. To claim that we know, or can know, with certainty, how a living organism will evolve in and with a particular environment is not science; it is arrogance *(hubris)*. Early in 1989, however, the U.S. Government approved field trials in Hawaii. $20 million or so later, in 1993, Calgene intends to have these tomatoes on the market in the U.S., every one of them with a little sticker saying "McGregor – grown from Flavr Savr seeds" – Flavr Savr being Calgene's trade name for its patented tomatoes. (Actually it is the genetic technology that is patented, but it does, perforce, extend to the tomato containing the technology.)

While agribusiness in one place is slowing down the aging process of tomatoes, in another it is working in the opposite direction. Union Carbide, of Bophal fame, markets a plant regulator called Ethrel. It is a versatile substance, used on tobacco, cherries, apples, and tomatoes, among other crops. The manufacturers recommend that Ethrel be applied when 5-30% of a tomato crop is pink or red and the rest 'mature green'. Two to three weeks later the entire crop can be harvested when it is uniformly ripe. What the drug does is cause "an early release of ethylene – nature's ripening agent". There is a problem, however, when this is applied to a crop of tomatoes destined for the retail market rather than processing. Because it speeds up ripening, the tomatoes keep speeding until they rot, which may be the day after you buy them. But spraying does get table tomatoes onto the early market, when the price is highest, quicker!

Another example is wheat as it is grown and wheat as it is consumed, probably thousands of miles away. Canadian wheat does not suffer anything like the intrusions, in the growing stage, that the potato does, but what happens to it post-harvesting is something else again. Fumigants and fungicides, deterioration due to moisture, and contamination in transport and storage, are just some of the things that affect the grain before it is even milled, to say nothing of what happens during and after milling. (Look at the ingredients on any loaf of factory bread. The wheat was an adequate food when it started out.)

Technically, the highly processed white bread may contain all the nutrients, according to available chemical analysis, of various forms of 'health' bread. But chemical analysis does not account for fibre, or texture, and like sociology, makes certain requirements of its samples. It can be argued that the analysis itself alters the substance being analyzed. Whether the human body values all the additives in the same way it would the whole grains is another question, and there are subtleties concerning micro-nutrients about which we still know very little. Interestingly enough, there has been a significant shift in public demand in North America towards more whole grain breads regardless of price. (See Chapter 15 for the story of the Prairie Tall Grass Bread Co.)

As the historic leader in the drive to industrial agriculture, the United States has opted for quantity over quality, production over consumption. This is reflected in its approach to grain handling and marketing, where U.S. standards are considerably lower than those of Canada and where blending – mixing some high quality wheat with much lower quality in order to get an acceptable standard – is the practice. The grain dealers love this approach because of the latitude it gives them, but their customers are not always so pleased with what they get, which may include screenings, gravel and water.

The Canadian Wheat Board, working with the Canadian Grain Commission, does ensure both grade and quality within grade. It is able to do this because by law the Canadian Wheat Board is the sole purchaser of wheat and barley for export, though the CWB works with both co-operative and private dealers in selling grains into the export market. Of course there are always the 'free-market' farmers who think they personally would be better off without the Wheat Board and the standards of the Canadian Grain Commission and couldn't care less what happens to anyone else. For years this very small minority has been used by the corporate traders, like Cargill, to attack the Wheat Board and its control of the market. Despite the clear objections of the majority of grain farmers and their marketing organizations, Tory Minister of Agriculture Charlie Mayer, claiming he was simply giving farmers some 'choice' about how they market their grain, made an arbitrary decision to allow barley, as of August, 1993, to be exported to the U.S. outside of CWB jurisdiction and without grading.

Quite apart from the questions of grain quality and nutrition is the question of the *structural* effects of new processing technology, such as Washburn's development of an air-separation technique for milling wheat in 1871. This new method enabled the high-protein (high gluten) hard spring wheat that grows well in the dry climate of the Great Plains of North America to be used to produce a pure white flour. This fine flour absorbs more water than the soft (lower gluten) winter wheats of the east, and thus gives bread made with it a longer shelf life.[18] This technological distancing in turn made concentration of the milling industry possible and gave the American millers a global advantage of scale and market reach over the Europeans who were still using the older techniques. (The French *baguette* cannot be made from flour milled by the Washburn technique. That is also why the French buy their bread fresh every day.)

While Canada still sees itself as the breadbasket of the world, there have been recent structural changes bringing more distance between its wheat and the bread eaters. In 1992 the U.S.-based transnational Archer Daniels Midland (ADM) purchased the Ogilvie Milling division of John Labatt Ltd. as well as McCarthy Milling from George Weston Ltd., while Maple Leaf Foods (owned by Hillsdown Holdings of Britain) and ConAgra

(USA) formed a partnership to operate their flour mills on both sides of the Canadian-US border. As a result, by the end of 1992 two U.S. companies (ADM and ConAgra) controlled 75-80% of Canada's aggregate milling capacity. Only two smaller companies, Dover Industries, Ltd., and B.P. Kent Flour Mills Ltd., are entirely Canadian owned.[19]

ENERGY INEFFICIENCY

Energy consumption by the food system increases as industrialization and distancing increase. The amount of energy required to produce a calorie of food is constantly increasing, meaning that the system is, by this measure, increasingly *inefficient*. In the early 1970s researchers calculated that more than ten kilocalories of energy subsidy are now required to produce one kilocalorie of food in the U.S. agricultural-food system, while most non-industrial societies' agricultural sectors are net energy *producers*. The energy inputs for industrial agriculture and its food system include nitrogen and its manufacture for fertilizer, agro-toxin manufacture, fuel for mechanized field work and transportation, refrigeration, etc.

When the cows lived near the people, and the horse that ate the grass along the road could deliver the milk fresh, without refrigeration, the energy consumption of the process was minimal. It is certainly not minimal now, and energy conservation plays little or no role in economic decision-making at the macro-level, although it will be a factor in individual enterprise decision-making.

> Herbicide, insecticide and fungicide sales worldwide in 1991 were roughly $26 billion, double the figure a decade earlier, with nearly $1 billion of those sales in Canada. The U.S. agro-toxin industry had domestic sales in 1992 of $6 billion and export sales of $2 billion.[20]

The Top Twelve Pesticide Makers, 1991 sales (millions of \$ US)[21]	
Ciba-Geigy, (Switzerland)	3,083
Imperial Chemical Industries (ICI) (Britain)	2,211
Bayer (Switzerland)	2,118
Rhône-Poulenc (France)	2,104
Du Pont (USA)	1,790
Dow Elanco (USA)	1,590
Monsanto (USA)	1,551
Hoechst (Germany)	1,480
BASF (Germany)	1,339
Schering (Germany)	1,003
American Cyanamid (USA)	900
Sandoz (Switzerland)	860
Total:	\$26,800,000,000

The current industrial-capitalist food system is efficient only according to corporate bookkeeping. The externalization of costs such as energy depletion, land degradation, water depletion and pollution, deforestation, loss of genetic resources, destruction of rural communities and, on top of it all, malnutrition, must lead the unbiased observer to the conclusion that the corporate accounting is simply fraudulent.

But fraudulent accounting is necessary to maintain the claim that a food system based on distancing is efficient, since every bit of distance is a cost.

Let us now turn to distancing where we experience it directly, at the supermarket.

CHAPTER 4

GOING SHOPPING

FEEDING CORPORATE CONCENTRATION

What we see when we go shopping for groceries has, until very
recently, depended very much on where we live. Smaller cities
and towns have presented a fairly uniform picture. Where there
is no substantial elite of wealth, and the poor are either hidden or
desperately attempting to be invisible in the lower middle class,
the food distribution system looks very much like that in any
number of other similar communities. In a town of 40,000 to
100,000, and maybe even double that, there will be one or more
fast-food strips (very similar to the 'golden mile' of new and used
car lots and accessory stores one can find on the edge of every
North American town and city) with the usual chain and franchise occupants: a handful of convenience stores that are also
either small chains, franchises or members of a buying group;
possibly a remaining genuine independent; and then the large
supermarkets, which range from 40,000 sq. feet to 100,000 sq.
feet and may carry up to 30,000 different items. The large supermarkets usually require a town of 40,000 for a base, and in a city
of 80,000 and up the market attracts competing supermarkets.
At the top of the pyramid there is a newcomer, the 'club' store
which requires a much higher density and/or distance for exploitation, and which can devastate a fair-sized city as effectively
as a neutron bomb.

The best known of these mega-stores in the U.S. are Price
Club, Costco and Wal-Mart, which also operates as Sam's Club (in

mid-1993, Price and Costco announced they would merge). Wal-Mart operates 1914 stores, including 40 Supercenters and 277 Sam's Club outlets, with overall sales in the year ending January 1993 of $55.5 billion and pre-tax profits of $3.17 billion! Of this $55.5 billion, 'groceries' accounted for $13.8 billion. (Kroger, with sales of $22 billion in its conventional supermarkets, is the largest North American grocery retailer.)

OLIGOPOLIZATION

In 1912, the Great Atlantic & Pacific Tea Company, one of the first food chains, completed the testing of a new idea, the one-man economy store that eliminated credit and delivery and reduced margins to increase volume. By 1930, A&P had 15,737 stores in the U.S. and chain stores altogether had 32% of the U.S. food market. The self-service system in food stores was initiated in 1916 by the Piggly-Wiggly stores in the U.S.[22]

In Canada, food retailing is dominated by a few large chains. At the head of the list is Loblaws (a unit of George Weston Ltd., with 1992 sales of $9.26 billion), which also ranks as 50th largest retailer in the world. Univa, another food retailer, ranks 71st on the global list complied in early 1993. According to a right-wing Canadian business magazine,

"Four Canadian companies now rank among the planet's top 100 retail chains, thanks mostly to this country's supermarket oligopoly." Loblaw Cos. Ltd. ranks as the 50th largest retailer in the world, followed by Univa, Inc., parent of the Provigo grocery chain, as 71st. Oshawa Group Ltd., known for its Food City and IGA supermarkets, is 96th. Wal-Mart Stores Inc. and K Mart Corp are ranked as the top two by Management Horizons of Columbus, Ohio. The average shopkeeper in the top 100 boasts more than 1900 outlets, sales of $10 billion, and profit of $240 million. The top 25 companies alone account for nearly half the list's sales and 79% of profit.[23]

The trade journal Canadian Grocer used to carry a monthly update on the sales and financial highlights of the major food wholesalers and retailers. Sometime in 1992 it gave this up, a comment on the fact that many of the companies once listed are now privately owned, such as Dominion or A&P, and statistics are no longer available, or they have become divisions of larger integrated entities that may be engaged in processing, wholesaling and retailing. The entire sector is now referred to as the PDR – Processing, Distribution, Retailing – sector. Even this category may need to be expanded to include the likes of Wal-Mart, which might be more aptly described as a merchandise broker selling to the public than as a food retailer, clothing store or auto-parts emporium.

It used to be that retailers went to their customers, locating their shops where people congregated for a variety of reasons, such as getting a hair cut and going to the post office (remember those days?) before picking up the groceries. Or they were located within easy walking of home, filling both the service and social role now relegated to the very marginal 'mom and pop' corner stores. Then the superstores came along, with their malls, pulling people out of their neighbourhoods and into dedicated merchandising locations. The next stage, led in Canada by Loblaws, which actually uses the name Superstore, was to build even bigger, free-standing stores even further from the centre of town. The even more mammoth new Wal-Mart facilities (Supercenters, they are being called, with 115,000 to 190,000 square feet of merchandising space) are what must be the final step in this progression, with people travelling literally tens and hundreds of kilometres to shop in these monsters that deal in such volume that they can dictate terms and prices to their suppliers. This is certainly true in food sales.

> Wal-Mart is sidestepping the stiffest competition by opening its Supercenters mostly in small towns. It's using them to replace the earliest Wal-Mart discount stores, which are in rural areas where founder Sam Walton originally wiped out his competition by offering lower prices and wider variety than local merchants could match.[24]

At the other end of the spectrum in the global distribution system are the highly automated, capital intensive convenience stores like the Japanese-owned chain 7 Eleven, where the vending machines, coffee makers and snack foods compete with and even resemble the video games. The social milieu of the video-violence is a far cry from what I remember of the corner drug store where I sometimes went with a friend for a soda after school!

The patterns of scale are familiar and logical enough, but how they are organized within the distribution and ownership structures is less visible. The big chains all have their standard supermarkets, such as Safeway (US and Canada), A&P (US and Canada) Loblaws (Canada and US), along with smaller affiliates. Increasingly there is little to distinguish between comparable-size stores, as each chain has its flagship stores (the price-setters) which it owns and operates directly, its franchise or affiliate stores that operate under a name such as Mr. Grocer, No Frills, New Dominion, Foodland, or Save-easy, and the 'independents' which have a purchasing agreement.

What you see within these merchandisers of food and other items has changed drastically since the 1950s when every store was uniformly dull and boring, with few concessions to visual attractiveness, and the air filled with engineered Muzak. Not so any more, except for the warehouse or bulk stores located in poorer neighbourhoods on the one hand and the Wal-Marts and Superstores on the other, where low price over-rides any consideration of aesthetics.

Now the soup cans and breakfast foods are lined up, like the cleaning aids and cookies, in the centre of the store, while around the periphery are a number of differentiated and apparently independent businesses. In rare cases they actually are. There may be flower shops and drug stores, delis and bakeries, lunch counters and gourmet food shops. The most sophisticated retailers have done away with the music altogether, softened the lighting and added a great deal of visual attractiveness through imaginative use of huge photographs, colour, and space configuration.

The vulgarity of marking prices on every package is rapidly being replaced with the sophistication of bar codes and electronic shelf markers. The prices displayed on these miniature radio receivers can be changed from the store office, enabling the marketing experts or the store manager to jiggle prices at will without all the hassle and expense of hiring night workers to change the prices manually. No more new price stickers over old ones, no more more consumer observation of the manipulation going on, no more after-school jobs for the teenagers. Price changes can be made at will on old and new stock on the shelf and at the check-out simultaneously. Without individual pricing, which certainly saves on labour (and tedious work) in the supermarket, when you get home and put your groceries away you can compare last week's price with what you just paid by consulting your cash register receipt – if you remembered to keep it. On the other hand, you will need a good calculator and a lot of patience to figure out just how much actual food you just purchased, as opposed to packaging, etc.

All the apparent diversity in presentation, range of products, packaging, cooking styles, and price, obscures the overall centralizing of control and the *distancing*. For example, Swiss-owned Nestlé (the world's largest food company with consolidated sales in 1992 of $37.3-billion) is recognized as a food company. It makes 200 different blends of its Nescafé brand coffee as one aspect of its diversity in supplying more than 300 brands of food products, emanating from 400 factories around the world, to stores in 160 countries.

Philip Morris, on the other hand, is known as a tobacco company. Founded in 1847, Philip Morris describes itself in one of its annual reports as "the world's largest packaged-consumer-goods company and largest tobacco company (excluding the monopoly industry in China)". Philip Morris only became a food company in 1985 when it purchased General Foods. Three years later it also purchased Kraft and combined the two into Kraft General Foods, the name you are most likely to see on its food products. In 1992 Philip Morris had consolidated sales of $59 billion, with tobacco accounting for $25.7 billion of the total and food $29 billion. The third largest food processor in the world behind Nestlé and Philip Morris is Unilever of Holland and Britain, with 1992 sales of $37 billion. (The discrepancies in descriptions and figures are the result of the complexity and diversity of these companies. It all depends on what you wish to see, or how they wish to be seen.)

PSEUDO-DIVERSITY

The size of the stores, and of the corporations behind them, makes global sourcing and apparent diversity a marketer's delight. For example, Loblaws' President's Choice private label line alone now includes 1000 items in Canada. The current rate of new foods introduction is 10-12,000 per year, with about two thirds of them disappearing (failing) within a year. Nearly 70% of the 15,886 food, household and personal care products introduced in 1992 were line extensions (modifications or versions of products already on the market).

> "In this decade, it is possible that more than 170,000 new food products will be introduced, and at least 20,000 of them could be 'significant'," meaning that they will receive substantial marketing support, according to *Gorman's New Product News* in Chicago.[25]

In smaller towns there is limited choice, overall, though there may be more variety in a large supermarket that is part of a chain. In larger urban centres there is not only more choice, there are also differences in what is available in different areas of the city. This is a reflection of ethnic diversity, but it is also a reflection of the distribution of wealth. In those areas where wealth is concentrated there may be many small shops specializing in one style or type of food, from meat to bakery, deli to fish, as well as a big lush supermarket. This consumer and product diversity, however, does carry with it a high price tag. It costs a whole lot more to carry six brands of apple juice than one.

In other parts of the city, where there is little disposable income, the old shops that used to serve the neighbourhoods are vacant, or house a steady succession of small shop-keepers with visions of independent success. Most of the money is spent in one of the few accessible large chain stores. Variety and attractiveness are not emphasized, and very often the prices are higher than in a neighbourhood where there is more mobility and experience of choice.

Because of different names, different colours, different labels, it is not immediately apparent that the distribution sector of the food system, and control of the products it sells, has been steadily concentrating into fewer and fewer hands. While it may look like there are a lot of retailers in competition with each other, it is more likely that each is functioning according to its allotted role in the system. Competition is very limited, as indicated by the great size and small number of major distributors:

FOOD RETAILERS IN CANADA	*(1992 sales, Can. $)* [26]	
Loblaw Cos.	$9.26 billion	Loblaws, Superstores, Zehrs,
retail	$6.42 b.	Fortinos, National (U.S.)
wholesale	$2.84 b.	
Univa	$6.7 billion	Provigo, Maxi (Que.);
		Loeb/IGA (Ont)
Oshawa Group	$5.01 billion	Food City, IGA, Dutch Boy,
		Price Chopper
Safeway	$4.36 billion	Safeway, Food For Less
A & P	$2.98 billion	A&P, Dominion, Miracle
		Mart
Métro-Richelieu	$2.31 billion	Métro-Richelieu, Super
		Carnaval (Quebec only)
Sobey's	$2.04 billion	Sobey's, Lofood, Calbeck
Overwaitea	$2.00 b.(+/-)	Overwaitea (BC)

Among the variety of ways the large corporations control the market is through the practice of differential pricing for identical products. The major distributors charge their own flagship stores the lowest prices, with their smaller chain stores (corporately owned or franchises) next up the price ladder. As the buyers get smaller and more removed from the corporate structure, the prices go up. The percentage differences may be as much as 15% between levels. The corner store is thus caught in a double-bind. In order to attract customers, it has to be provide convenience and variety. That means it has to be open longer hours than the major stores, making it very labour intensive. At the same time it has to charge considerably higher prices than the corporate stores to cover the much higher prices it pays for its goods. There is little likelihood of a small store growing up into a big store any more.

This distribution and pricing structure has had tragic consequences in some cities, such as Los Angeles, where the prices charged by convenience stores in depressed neighbourhoods are seen as price gouging and exploitation. The stores, very often run by Asian immigrants and their families, have come under attack by other racial groups on these grounds, transforming the issue of capitalist structure into one of racial conflict.

> Many food and hardware chains use a host of special fees and discounts when buying merchandise from their suppliers. . . If the suppliers refuse to co-operate, they can lose the business or find their products relegated to the bottom shelf. These special 'allowances' are a real threat to suppliers in a country like Canada where a handful of supermarket chains control more than 90% of all the food sold in the country, industry officials have said. . . Few suppliers are powerful enough to stand up to the supermarket chains. . . Food suppliers may not like the supermarket's negotiating practices, but there is little they can do about it.[27]

Nestlé, Unilever, Wal-Mart, Philip Morris, RJR Nabisco, Weston/Loblaws, A&P each have their core strengths: two in tobacco, one strictly in ruthless merchandising, one in the integration of retailing, wholesaling and processing, and two in food manufacturing. These are the major forces in the PDR sector, the players that we are apt to meet most frequently when we go grocery shopping. We may not see their names, but if we look closely we will find their identities. For example, the address of Sunfresh at 22 St. Clair Ave. E., Toronto, is a clue to the Weston empire, for this is the address of their modest office building that is the business address of all their companies. Look carefully for the identities of the controlling interests the next time you go shopping.

The overlap, or integration, of manufacturing, processing and distribution, makes it extremely difficult to provide a tidy or even accurate profile of the entire sector. Compare the table of 'food processors' on the next page with the list of 'food retailers'.

FOOD PROCESSORS IN CANADA [28]

	1991 sales $billions Can.	ownership
John Labatt Ltd.	$5.370	public, Brascan 39%, Caisse 11%
Maple Leaf Foods Ltd.	$3.035	public, Hillsdown Holdings 56%
McCain Foods Ltd.	$2.700	private, McCain family
Geo. Weston Ltd.	$2.088	public, W.G Weston 57%
Kraft General Foods	$1.649	private, Phillip Morris 100%
Co-op Federée	$1.249	co-op, private
Agropur	$1.028	co-op, private
Nestlé	$ .964	private, Nestlé SA 100%
Beatrice Foods	$ .834	private, Merrill Lynch 100%
Nabisco Brands Ltd.	$ .770	private, RJR Nabisco 100%
Unilever	$ .688	private, Unilever PLC. 100%
H.J. Heinz Ltd.	$ .459	private, H. J. Heinz Co. 100%
Campbell Soup Co.	$ .448	private, Campbell Soup Co.100%
Cargill (meat only)	$ .275	private, Cargill Inc. 100%

It is well known, and oft repeated by the companies in public, that operating margins in food distribution are very low, at 1 or 2%. However, what it seldom mentioned, and never in the same breath, is that inventory turnover runs 11.8 to 17.5 times per year, providing a return on capital of 12–30%! These figures go far toward explaining the high stakes in the game and the tendencies toward oligopoly.

'Consumer demand', distribution efficiency, and increased control may seem like cause enough to move the food distribution sector in the direction it is going, but the drive to reduce labour costs is also a major factor. Apart from using the buying power they may have, either as very large enterprises in themselves, as integrated food processors-distributors, or as members of buying clubs, about the only area of flexibility that exists for most retail stores is labour costs. Given the fact that most of us in North America are not going to significantly increase the amount of food we eat, and that there is simply no more room for yet more profitable stores, market share can only be increased by driving someone else out of business through lowering costs and prices or offering better service, however that is perceived. In a static economy this all adds up to pressure on wages, so it is not surprising that the corporations with the clout are now seeking concessions from unionized labour and ways around having union labour at all. Since it is the retail end of food distribution that is labour intensive, it can be franchised out or sold to independent operators who remain tied to the suppliers. When this escape route is not possible, the alternative is an attack on wages, as illustrated by recent moves by A&P and Nestlé.

In early 1993, unionized employees at Safeway have voted to accept the wage concessions negotiated by their unions. Wages for clerks will drop from $18.14 to $16.04 per hour while cashiers will drop from $17.25 to $15.22. Full-time workers face a $30 a week drop in pay but work three hours longer. Part-time workers will drop $40 while working three hours longer.

After being without a contract since the end of January, 1993, 220 members of the Retail, Wholesale and Department Store Union were locked out of the Chesterville, Ontario plant of Nestlé Canada Inc. when they voted against the company offer. The new contract would have given them a 2% wage increase over the current average wage of $15 the first year and three years inflation protection after that. The real issue, however, was the company's insistence that it needed a 'continental work week' with no premium for weekend work, like the other Nestlé plants. This would mean an end to time and a half on Saturday and double time on Sunday. The company said it would transfer production of instant coffee, powdered chocolate, juice and pudding products to plants in the U.S. or Mexico if the workers did not accept the company offer.

Nestlé Canada president Michael Rosicki sent a letter to the employees of the Chesterville Factory, March 19, 1993, addressed "Dear fellow employee" in which he advised that "Whether we like it or not, Nestlé Canada is now part of a North American market and we at Nestlé must strive to become more competitive in this market. . . Nestlé currently has too many factories in North America. . . A Nestlé Coffee Task Force has been established to study the situation and determine the best way to produce coffee in North America. The Task Force will recommend expanding, down-sizing or closing factories as necessary. Who wins and who loses will be decided on the basis of which factories are the most competitive. . . These are the fundamental changes to your previous contract. . . I'm sure you understand the implications of these negotiations, if you choose to reject our offer, the consequences are clear."[29]

In May the 220 production workers voted to accept a four-year collective agreement in which Nestlé agreed to limit the continental work week to the 40 unionized workers on the plant's instant coffee production line, pay each worker a lump-sum signing bonus, and give them an annual cost-of-living wage increase.

FAST BUCKS AND TAKEOVERS

The powers of oligopoly and the concentration of wealth characteristic of the food business in the 1980s, whether expressed through wage settlements, slotting fees, buying power, or just plain profits, made the PDR sector an attractive battlefield for take-over-and-break-up fast-buck artists like Michael Milken or the firm of Kohlberg Kravis Roberts (KKR).

The technique they developed and exploited is the leveraged buyout, a process whereby someone with a bit of cash borrows whatever amount necessary, using the acquired company's own capital as collateral, to buy a profitable business. The buyer then issues bonds in the name of the 'new' company (referred to as 'junk bonds' because they have so little collateral and so much debt behind them, requiring them to carry a very high rate of interest to attract speculators), to raise the cash to repay the loans with which they had purchased the company in the first place. The issue is control, and the leveraged buyout illustrates how a ruthless opportunist can gain control of a very large prosperous company with very little real money. The cash cow is then furiously milked and burdened with horrendous debts.

The era of leveraged buyouts got under way in 1986 when Kohlberg Kravis Roberts bought out Beatrice Foods in the U.S. for $6.2 billion (only on paper, of course). A year later, KKR bought Safeway for $4.2 billion in another leveraged buyout, but very quickly had to begin breaking up Beatrice and selling off pieces of it to cover the interest on its debt/junk bonds. One of the pieces broken off of Beatrice was its Canadian operations, which were bought, in another leveraged buyout, by Onex Corporation of Toronto.

Of course none of this had anything to do with food as such, or with the needs of most people. Food was simply a means of accumulating wealth in a very big hurry. The manipulations contributed nothing to the 'efficiency', 'productivity', or 'competitiveness' of the businesses themselves and ultimately pushed the costs of excessive interest rates and capital gains onto the individual consumers through the prices paid for their food.

But Beatrice was only the beginning. In 1988, while Philip Morris was buying Kraft (for $13.1 billion) and combining it with General Foods, KKR was busy arranging another leveraged buyout, this time of RJR Nabisco, which had been formed in 1985 when R.J. Reynolds Tobacco bought Nabisco Foods, for a record $25 billion. The four investment banks working for KKR stood to get at least $400-million in fees out of the deal and since that time RJR Nabisco has been trying to pay off the debt that had been loaded onto it.

With KKR still controlling Nabisco with 49% of its common shares, by early 1993 the debt had been reduced from a peak of $30 billion to $14 billion. This means that the consumers of Nabisco products have paid down the $16 billion. (You try to figure out the 'tax' on each product!) In 1992 the food businesses of RJR Nabisco had sales of $6.71 billion with earnings of $947 million.[30]

BRAND NAMES AND NEW NAMES

If big-name food companies made attractive targets for the quick-buck boys in the 1980s, in the 1990s it seems to be the name brands they are going after. The issue is, once again, capturing control of whatever aspect of the food system seems to be making the most money. If Proctor & Gamble or Nabisco or Kraft General Foods seems to be getting too much of your food dollar with its name brands, you can be sure that someone else, like Loblaws or Wal-Mart, will go after that piece of the business. The result is 'President's Choice' (PC) and, now, 'Sam's American Choice' (although Sam Walton died a year ago) – complete with an American flag, just in case you doubted Walton's loyalty.

> Incremental price hikes on many branded food items through the 70s and 80s left a major price void which private label manufacturers jumped into with a vengeance. Retail price differentials between branded and private label products generally range from 30 to 50%. A lot of the large branded manufacturers have focused their entire marketing mechanism toward pleasing Wall Street first, toward short-term profit... In the case of Loblaws, Canada's largest retailer and wholesaler of grocery products, Loblaw-controlled brands account for 32% of the company's Canadian dollar sales and 37% of its unit sales.[31]

There is one more piece of the PDR sector that must be mentioned since it appears, sadly but not surprisingly, to be a growing segment of the food system: food banks and other charity/welfare provisions for those marginalized out of, or excluded from, the marketplace.

In March, 1993, there were 27.38 million people living in the U.S. participating in the federal food stamp program. That is about 10% of the population, and the largest number ever, having increased by more than 4.4 million since March 1991. These figures do not take into account those dependent on the federal WIC (women, infants and children) or school lunch programs, to say nothing of state or local programs.

In Canada, where there are no federal food programs, the slack gets taken up by the general welfare system and the charity system of food banks. By and large these operate as extensions of the corporate distribution system.

> According to the director of grocery procurement for Loblaws Supermarkets Ltd., prior to Loblaws' association with the food banks damaged products were sold on the dollar to an outside agent or a discount division, and while the company would be rid of the product, the aggravation and time spent finding a place for those goods was nightmarish. The food banks are a far more efficient way to get rid of the product [because they] simply pick up the goods or the company delivers them... In fact, food banks are rapidly coming to be regarded as a good

way to move perishable food that, if left for longer, would simply end up in a landfill.[32]

About 70% of food-bank donations – about 13 million kilograms a year – comes from food manufacturers and distributors. . . For industry, handing excess over to a food bank creates goodwill and avoids dumping fees.[33]

FARMING BY FRANCHISE

> Maple Leaf Foods (formerly Canada Packers) Agribusiness Group companies includes pork and poultry processing operations, as well as Shur-Gain feeds. According to their Annual Report, in 1992 they extended their 'Partnership Program', so that "the various operations of the Agribusiness Group are able to offer a tailored package of their many products and services to customers and farmers on a one-stop shopping basis."

Business is business, as they say, whether in food, tractors or agro-toxins. What is happening at the retail end of the system is also happening at the farm end. Farm input suppliers have consolidated and the farmer, like the consumer, engages in one-stop shopping, buying fertilizer, chemicals, and seeds from one supplier that may be owned by a transnational corporation (TNC) that produces the herbicides and pesticides and the seeds and the fertilizer, like Cargill or ICI.[34] These same corporations engage in biotechnology research with the aim of transforming the seed into a carrier of certain patented genes, which make the plant tolerant of (or resistant to) the herbicide manufactured by the same company. Or the seed may be coated with the chemicals required to sustain the seed in its infancy until the application of externally supplied life-support products can be undertaken in accordance with the manufacturer's specifications.

At harvest time, the purchaser of the resulting 'rural product' may be the same corporation that supplied all the inputs, or it may be a processor of that product, whether a meat packer, miller, french-fry manufacturer, canner, or produce distributor who will stipulate the treatments and harvesting dates and methods not already governed by the input supplier.

For example, a potato farmer in Manitoba who sells his potatoes to Carnation (which is owned by Nestlé) gets a lower price for organic, or non-chemical, potatoes "because the chemically grown potatoes *cook whiter*". Carnation is *the* french fry supplier for McDonald's in Canada. In the same way, a New Brunswick potato farmer gets a premium from Humpty Dumpty depending on the 'whiteness' of the potato he delivers. Another farmer may have a contract with McCain's, in which case the farmer may well purchase fertilizer and seed potatoes from McCains, machinery from McCain's subsidiary, Thomas Equipment, finance his crop through McCain's, and then deliver the crop to McCain's, if they will accept it.

After Cargill Ltd. bought Maple Leaf Mills' grain division in 1988 and started its visible expansionist wave in Canada, it issued an information sheet for Ontario farmers advising them of the services Cargill was prepared to offer through its 23 newly-acquired feed mills in south western Ontario:

> Cargill's purpose remains to provide essential goods and services to meet human needs. . . Cargill offers farmers a complete line of services and crop inputs. Cargill sells herbicides, fertilizers and chemicals, rents out applicators and helps with soil tests. . . We offer farmers a balanced marketing program for their grains. . . Cargill is a leader in the marketing of farm commodities. . . Cargill produces top-quality, custom-made and standard rations for livestock and poultry.

Like their counterparts at the other end of the system, Cargill's customers and its 'franchised' farmers are expected to follow directions carefully. The farmer, like the retail franchisee, must also assume the risks that the corporations wish to avoid, in this case the risks of weather, the risks of spoilage and bad temper, the necessity of selling the product when it is ready because it has no value otherwise and cannot be stored, and the problems of labour, whether their own or that of others. One way of dealing with the cost-price squeeze is super-exploitation of workers who are in a situation where they have to take what they are offered.

It is often assumed that Canadian agriculture mimics that of the U.S.A. If this were so, we should expect to find corporate farming taking over in Canada as it has done particularly in the south east and south west of the U.S.A. But our conditions are different, and perhaps the greatest difference, apart from weather, is the lack of a large reserve of cheap labour, such as agri-business has access to in Mexico or in the large numbers of 'undocumented' workers in the U.S.A., i.e., illegal immigrants from the countries south of the border. Canada does use some migrant labour, but on nothing like the scale of the U.S.A.

Agribusiness gets around the labour 'problem' by gaining control of every aspect of the food system where labour can be more easily controlled or marginalized than in primary production or some areas of retailing. Thus agribusiness has gained virtually total control over agricultural inputs as well as agricultural outputs, i.e. the processing and distribution of food. The independence of the farm unit is itself illusory. The deed to the farm may carry the farmer's name, but it will be a bank or the Farm Credit Corporation that holds the mortgage. Farmers may buy their inputs in their own name, but they may well be bought on credit supplied either by the dealer or by the purchaser of the farm crop, if they are not already one and the same (as is often the case in monoculture production like potatoes, tomatoes, corn or even beef).

Poultry is the most obvious area of vertical integration in the U.S., though hogs are coming up fast. The 'integrators,' like ConAgra, Tyson, Cargill and a few others in the U.S., or Maple Lodge Farms in Canada, own the feed companies, supply the chicks (or piglets) and the feed, and buy the grown birds (or hogs) for slaughter and processing. They may well also supply feed consultant and veterinary services and a how-to manual. The hybrid (or patented) breeding stock may also be owned by the integrator or a franchised supplier. The packing plant (killing and processing) is always owned by the integrator, and it is from this perspective that the system is operated. The integrator will supply birds to KFC (Kentucky Fried Chicken – the 'Fried' is now being dropped as unhealthy) or some other large buyer according to their specifications.

What the farmer as an 'independent' operator is left with is the high-risk, relatively labour-intensive area of managing the live birds or pigs or the equally capital intensive and high-risk monoculture production of wheat or corn. This is virtually identical to the operation of a fast-food franchise, and while there are certainly a few winners under this system, there is an increasing number of losers, though the business press seldom reports on these.

Suppliers and buyers at both ends work on a cost-plus basis: that is, the cost of materials, labour, and capital, plus a profit, while the franchisee is strung out between fixed input costs and prices over which he or she has no control. (In the case of poultry, the Canadian supply-management marketing boards do ensure an adequate return to the operator, but the structure is still as described.) Given this set-up, there is no reason to expect that corporations dedicated to profit should want to move directly into on-farm food production. Their desire to franchise retailing and concentrate on processing, distribution and wholesaling is based on the same logic.

In 1986, 40% of Canada's retail trade of $44-billion was conducted through franchises and affiliated franchise-type businesses employing some 300,000 people. One franchise association estimated that by 1990, 75% of retail trade would be conducted through franchise companies. They were, apparently, a little too enthusiastic, both about franchising and about the economy. In 1992 there were some 500 franchise systems operating in Canada, but they still accounted for only 40% of the retail business, with annual revenues of more than $80 billion.[35]

> McDonald's and Burger King are the two biggest fast-food chains in the world. McDonald's has 643 franchise and corporate outlets in Canada (395 and 248 respectively), 8814 establishments in the U.S., and 3154 in the rest of the world. Burger King has 179 outlets in Canada (106 and 73 respectively), 5500 in the U.S. and 721 elsewhere. 5738 franchised restaurants and 1283 food retailing establishments are members of the Canadian Franchise Association, and together these establishments had revenues of $3.9 billion.[36]

Genuine diversity will be traded off for uniform variety from coast to coast coupled with centralized control. The Taco Bell in St. John's will be identical to that in Edmonton, Lafayette Indiana, or Mexico City. And all will contribute to the wealth of PepsiCo, the owner of the Taco Bell franchise.

Another illustration of the franchise principle can be seen in the area of farm finance. In North America banks and insurance companies and others own huge amounts of farm land, but they do not farm. It is common for a farmer to go bankrupt and have the farm seized by the creditor, who then leases the land back to the same farmer. The creditors know that this is advantageous because no one will work harder than that farmer or exploit his or her own labour more. This practice is reinforced by the creditors knowing that if they put the land on the market, it will depress land prices and thus reduce their equity. So they keep title to the land, as speculators, and lease it out to those who have some commitment to the land.

> The major insurance companies in the United States held over 5-million acres of farmland in 1987. The farms were valued at $2.7-billion and the mortgages valued at $9.2-billion.[37]

> In 1992 there were 191 farm bankruptcies in the Province of Saskatchewan alone and by February, 1993, financial institutions held 1.67 million acres of farmland out of the province's total of 65 million acres of farmland or 50 million acres of 'improved' farmland. The total outstanding agricultural debt in Saskatchewan alone at the end of 1992 was $5 billion, and the total Canadian farm credit outstanding was $23.8 billion. This includes credit outstanding from banks, the Farm Credit Corporation and other lending agencies, supply companies, etc.[38]

Of course, what gets played on at every turn is the image of the farmer as an independent entrepreneur. The franchisee is manipulated in the same fashion: "You've got a great place in a prime location, but business is bad. Your concept is tired, and it's time for a change." So reads an ad for a franchise, but it could be for a farm just as easily as for a restaurant.

A "professional agrologist and consultant" has described the modern farmer this way:

> A farmer is a buyer of land, buildings, machinery, equipment, livestock, semen, quota, feed, minerals, vitamins, hormones and other additives, medicines, seed, fertilizer, insecticides, fungicides, herbicides, small tools, crop insurance, fire insurance, liability insurance, car insurance, workman's compensation, futures, and many other varied items.[39]

The image this conveys is hardly that of a steward of the

land, a tiller of the soil, but it is the image that the 'modern' agricultural establishment has spent millions to sell to farmers around the world.

It is not unreasonable to assert that the farmer is being deliberately alienated from the profession of agri*culture* and recruited to a job and class position that allies the farmer with agribusiness management in the same way that the food retailer and even the consumer become functions of agribusiness. All are supposed to meet the expectations nurtured by agribusiness advertising and promotion. The farmer who cannot command the resources to play the game is dismissed as a 'bad manager', while the person who does not command the resources to buy the processed products of the system cannot be a 'valued customer'.

It all adds up to alienation, or another form of distancing.

"When Fishery Products International of Newfoundland had to find a replacement for northern cod, it bought from Alaskan freezer ships. The fish were then shipped to China to be processed and sold back to North America. That's global competition!" This is according to Cedric Ritchie, chairman of Scotia Bank, approvingly quoted in Toronto's national paper for business, the *Globe and Mail*. It might better be described, however, as a horrible example of phenomenally inefficient distancing.

CHAPTER 5

INDUSTRIAL FOOD

INDUSTRIALIZED LIVESTOCK

At one end of the long windowless barn the 75,000 chicks go in. Halfway along the barn are steel feed bins. Large trucks periodically turn up to blow five or ten tonnes of feed into the bins. The feed is moved by auger and conveyor into the barn and onto the chicks' dinner plate. Out the far end, weeks later, come the broilers. On another farm with apparently identical buildings, young hens go in, and out the other end come eggs and, at less frequent intervals, ' spent' hens, which go to the soup company for recycling.

To say simply that *industrialization* describes the transformation of farming and the food system in the latter half of the 20th century obscures the fact that ideology and special interests were the driving force of this industrialization. Equated with the notion of Progress, and therefore largely unchallenged, industrialization continues to be a major tool of distancing.

Several processes combined, as they did in other sectors, to bring about the current form of agriculture in North America and Europe: the substitution of capital for labour; the application of the concepts of efficiency and productivity as the key measurements of success; the application of technology; and, the adoption of modern accounting practices, meaning the measurement of the enterprise in terms of cash flow and profit.

The ideology of industrialization *reifies* (from the Latin word for 'thing') farming just as it reifies food; that is, both food and farming become *things*, their subsequent value to be determined by The Market, not by whether they husband the land and feed the population. Descriptions of short-term productivity and narrowly conceived efficiency reveal very little about how the farm is really doing or how healthy the children are.

The wholesale application of the type of technology advocated and developed within the social context of reductionist science and the industrial revolution (see Chapter 12) has created tremendous problems for farmers. These range from the degradation of the land through the use of chemical fertilizers, pesticides, heavy machinery, monoculture, irrigation and cash cropping, to the creation of human isolation and stress through the minimalization of labour, and the financial pressure to continually become more 'efficient' as a response to factors beyond the farmer's control.

Since the general public is now expressing some doubts about the whole process and seeks healthier food that is produced under more healthy conditions, it is essential to understand the bind the farmer has been put in, partly by choice and partly in response to external forces.

The transformation of agriculture into agribusiness occurred slowly and apparently for good purposes. The technological changes brought relief from arduous labour and, to a point, improved the quality of food. Technology applied to food preservation and transportation freed masses of people from rural toil and enabled them to move to the urban centres, where the toil took different forms. It also made possible the concentration of population, industry, and commerce that had been impossible previously because there was no practical way to feed a large urban population.

The argument as to whether it was the mechanization of agriculture that pushed people off the farms and into the industrial labour force, or the attraction of urban industrial employment that pulled them off the farms and required the mechanization of agriculture, does not need to be settled here. The results were the same, either way. Agriculture has industrialized at the same pace as the rest of the society. There was nothing unique about the process.

Chicken is cheap, cheap. It is the most highly industrialized meat we consume, and it is cheap at this point because of that. Not only has the production of chickens and eggs been turned into a production line process, the structure of the industry – and in this case the word does apply – itself is industrial, that is, integrated into a tightly controlled mechanized system. From the public standpoint, probably the most important question now is the quality of the product, but the public cannot raise that question without also being willing to consider the question of the price of the product. If one expects, or demands cheap food, then one cannot make contrary demands upon the producer. If the public wants healthy food, that is, food that is health producing for the consumer, for the producer, and for Creation, (whether that be chickens, land, or the people involved in production), then the price to the producer as well as the consumer must reflect that.

For example, intensively-raised animals of all sorts are prone to a host of parasites, and in the case of poultry, coccidiosis is a major problem, dealt with by the routine addition of a coccidiostat (a toxin) to the water. (A different culture might describe sub-therapeutic antibiotics or coccidiostats as potions to ward off the evil spirits of industrial food production.) Some microorganisms, such as coccidiosis and salmonella, thrive in a densely populated environment, being able to fulfil their life cycles with great ease and high rates of survival.

Salmonella is a curse specializing in poultry, under current circumstances. It has become such a problem, in fact, that the public, at least in the United States, is being told not to eat sunnyside-up eggs (eggs fried one side only, that is, not turned over). In fact, there are jurisdictions where it is now against the law for restaurants to serve eggs sunnyside-up. The problem, a good example of distancing, is real (though not new) and appears to arise from the high protein ingredients of chicken feed and the extremely close quarters under which industrial poultry is raised and eggs produced. Chickens, and their eggs, seem to be determined to be contaminated with salmonella under the present factory system of production.

Since the whole poultry production process has been centralized and industrialized, from feed production on to the egg or bird for slaughter, it seems that getting the salmonella out of the industrial process is virtually impossible. The only solution is to literally cook to death all poultry products (or irradiate them, yet another pseudo-solution to a real problem) – or de-industrialize and dismember poultry production as well as the bird itself. Salmonella is "the price we pay for the mass production of protein foods," as one food scientist concluded; and Britain's *New Scientist* magazine commented, "Only a well-coordinated campaign, launched by government simultaneously on several fronts, and with legal clout, can make our factory food safe. The bacteria are not running scared."[40]

Animals die when stressed beyond a certain point, and very often this stress is brought about by crowding – whether in chicken barn, hog barn, or beef feedlot – which is an essential function of industrialization. For example, on our farm we built a new barn one year, and moved a group of our pregnant ewes into it about three weeks before lambing. They started having abortions, and we had every aborted lamb autopsied by the provincial pathology lab. No cause could be identified, and the cause of death was finally labelled 'new barn syndrome' by the pathology lab. (We used to joke about 'dead chicken syndrome' when hens would keel over and die for no particular reason.) The only unusual thing we had done was to take a certain number of pregnant ewes from an open yard and confine them in a new, totally clean space in a newly built barn. We figured out later that we had put about three too many sheep in that space for their emotional and mental tranquillity at a crucial point in their pregnancy, although we had exceeded the space allotment recommended by the textbooks and government manuals. We thought we were being very respectful of their delicate condition. Their abortions were not an expression of disease, but a form of protest at the lack of adequate psychological space.

Modern confinement hog production is very similar. A routine sub-therapeutic (low) level of antibiotic feeding is essential to counter the effects of stress. If the public does not like this use of antibiotics, then it is not enough to demand that the farmer be prohibited from using them. The whole production system will have to be changed, just as it is already changing for poultry in some European countries under public pressure. In the short term costs will increase, costs the public must bear if it chooses to make such demands. But there are alternatives: I've seen hogs in Sweden that spend virtually the entire year outside and farrow (give birth) outside in deep straw litter in the coldest of temperatures. No need for drugs there.

A potentially far more disastrous disease has emerged more recently, again in Britain, that might yet undo the entire industrial food system. BSE *(bovine spongiform encephalopathy)* is referred to in Britain as 'mad cow disease' because of the behaviour of the cow prior to death. Mad cow disease was first observed on a British farm in 1985 and officially identified a year later as a form of spongiform encephalopathy (the name refers to the physical deterioration of the brain, making it look like a sponge). While first insisting it was caused by a virus or 'virus-like' agent, eventually the authorities had to recognize that whatever it is, the agent is not a bacteria or virus, so it has remained just that, an 'agent'. The 'agent' was originating, it appeared – and as far as the cows were concerned – in the protein concentrate being included in cattle feed. But then there was the question of where it was coming from before that. The answer turned out to be that it was coming from the rendered by-products of meat processing, including 'downer' cows and other cattle organ meat (offal). In other words, the cows were being forced to be cannibals, being fed, without their knowledge, rendered portions of probably unhealthy members of their own species. Not a healthy practice under any circumstances![41]

But there is much more to the story, because the disease seems to have a lot in common with scrapie, which has been known in sheep for centuries, and Creutzfeldt-Jakob disease in humans, identified first in 1920. It now appears highly likely that it is the same 'agent' in all three species, even though science has maintained, until very recently, that it is *not possible* for such an agent to cross species barriers.

For our purposes here, the point of the story is that in the name of productivity and efficiency, traditional and moral barriers to certain practices, such as feeding animals on the flesh and organs of their own species, were ignored. It would now appear that science has played a less than honourable or objective role in the whole affair, which is far from over.

Industrial agriculture is based on the premise that we can, with impunity, reconstruct creation according to our ideology. When chickens die by the thousands when the power goes off and the fans stop running, when pigs start chewing on each other's ears or tails because of overcrowding, or when sheep mysteriously abort, we cannot necessarily fix it with modern technology or drugs. (There are human analogies, too.)

> Frustrated by unexplained high poultry mortality rates, low pay and the indifferent attitude of Tyson Foods Inc., McCurtain County growers called in the Packers and Stockyards Administration to investigate their problems. Growers have seen their daily mortality go from 10 birds per house per day to 100 birds and more per house.
>
> For more than a year now each grower has been told by the company (Tyson) tech reps that it was an isolated problem on his farm and was the result of his bad management practices, although he was never told what he should be doing differently . . . When Packers & Stockyards investigators advertised a meeting with the growers, more than 80 growers came with records in hand.[42]

When the milk from young, high-producing cows undergoes what is called auto-oxidation and develops an 'off' taste, the best answer is not necessarily the vet's: large doses of Vitamin E. On the contrary. As one farmer thought about the problem with his own herd he realized that the milk in question was coming from those cows being pushed the hardest. As he thought about the various conditions and circumstances, he was led to suggest to the technicians and veterinarians that the problem did not lie within the cows. Instead he described the milk as 'immature', as having been pushed through the cow so fast that the cell structure actually was still immature when the milk came out, with the result that it broke down under stress, that is, when agitated, or exposed to air. Vitamin E, an anti-oxidant, might compensate for the problem, but it would not solve it. The solution lay in husbandry and feeding, and in understanding the natural processes at work that had their own rules and limits.

Husbandry and traditional extensive livestock feeding – grazing, use of farm-produced crops, etc. – is a very complex system essentially beyond the control of the purveyors of farm inputs: the drug and chemical companies. Allowing the milk to mature in the cow will provide benefits only to the farmer and the consumer (healthy cows and healthy milk), not to multinational corporations and their sales staff. That the agricultural scientists looked for external solutions to an on-farm problem reflects the current realities of the food system and the domination of reductionist thinking.

Any major change in this production system will require an ideological and philosophical shift away from the notion that we can and must control nature. Yet this is precisely the premise of industrial capitalist agriculture: that we can do what we want and impose our concepts and our rules on other species and on our environment with the assurance that any problems encountered or created along the way can be rectified with yet another technological fix.

Vandana Shiva of India provides a telling description of this ideology applied worldwide, in this case by the World Bank:

> For the World Bank everything works in terms of money. So if there is scarcity, what you do is generate more cash flows and somehow everything will take care of itself. . . All they see is that there are farmers in Canada and the USA producing surplus grain, and therefore what you need to do is create some sort of buying power on the part of other countries, other groups, to sort it all out. What they don't realize is that there is a way in which you can colonize people, colonize soils, and translate these into money by over-exploitation, and through that you can colonize the future.
>
> What they don't realize is that you can't do the reverse process. You can't have cash flows that will suddenly create soil fertility, money that will bring to life dead streams or bring water to dead wells. They don't realize that nature doesn't get created by money but it can get destroyed for generating money. That is where the logic of the banker is collapsing. They think they can play god, that they can restructure nature, and they think that all the problems of scarcity today, which are problems of the scarcity of nature to produce food and

scarcity of humans as part of nature to take care of her needs, are problems that they will be able to solve as bankers through money, cash flows, investments, and returns on investments.[43]

PSEUDO-DIVERSITY

> Genetic erosion eats away at the foundations of the world's food supply. It occurs when a few modern varieties displace the myriad varieties that once patchworked farmers' fields. High-yielding rice, for example, has conquered Asia. In some places, such as the Philippines, Indonesia and Vietnam, a single variety may account for as much as 60% of all rice production. In doing so, it sweeps aside hundreds of locally adapted varieties.[44]

Walking into any fair-sized supermarket might lead you to believe that diversity really is one of the consequences of the industrial food system. Whether it is the number of brands and qualities of toilet paper (all originating with one or two species of trees), the number of different kinds of fruits and vegetables in the produce section, or the flavours of potato chips and soft drinks, there certainly does seem to be plenty of variety. Choice – or 'freedom of choice' as right-wing ideology has it – seems to be a driving goal.

Unfortunately, as far as genetics goes, exactly the reverse is the case, and uniformity is the rule.

For example, even though there are 2000 species of potato in the *genus solanum*, all the potatoes grown in the United States, and most of those grown commercially everywhere else, belong to one species, *solanum tuberosum*. Twelve varieties of this one species constitute 85% of the U.S. potato harvest, but the one variety most favoured by the processors, the Russet Burbank, is by far the dominant variety. By 1982, 40% of the potatoes planted in the U.S. were Russet Burbanks.[45]

McDonald's Corporation in Britain is switching from the Pentland Dell variety of potato to the Russet Burbank because, "it is a more suitable potato for our requirements". McDonald's uses 55,000 tons of potatoes a year in Britain.[46]

Other major crops provide similar examples of the narrow genetic base of our food system. Although there are more than 250 varieties of wheat available, in 1981 six varieties accounted for nearly 40% of United States' wheat acreage while only four varieties of rice accounted for 65% of the rice acreage; six for 42% of the soybean land; three for 76% of the snap beans planted; two for 96% of the peas; and nine for 95% of the peanuts.[47]

In Canada, four varieties of wheat produce 75% of the crop grown on the Prairies and more than half of it comes from a single variety, Neepawa.

Appearances would suggest that there is a constantly increasing variety of both raw and processed food in our food system, but the fact of the matter is that the industrialized agriculture of North America has been systematically reducing genetic variety in the food system – both in number of species and in varieties within species – while increasing the apparent variety of what is referred to in the trade as 'product', whether this be in seed corn or corn flakes, strains of wheat or varieties of bread, types of cows or qualities of cheese, potatoes or potato chips. Where once the global food supply was derived from 3000-4000 different crops, we are now dependent on 20 or 30![48]

A reflection of this is found in the declining numbers of small independent seed companies. The Seed Saver Exchange of Iowa found that out of 230 companies inventoried in 1984, 54 were no longer in business in 1987. Between 1987 and 1991, 41 more companies disappeared, but during this period 49 new companies appeared, and many of these, like Salt Spring Seeds in British Columbia, are devoted to open-pollinated and heritage varieties. The larger established companies prefer hybrids and patented seeds because the gardener cannot save seed from these plants for the next year, either because they will not breed true, in the case of hybrids, or because the gardener would have to pay royalties, in the case of patented seed.

Seed Saver found that 943 open-pollinated varieties available in 1984 were no longer available from seed companies in 1987, and between 1987 and 1991, 1263 more varieties of open-pollinated vegetable seed (23.8% of the catalogued varieties) were dropped from the seed company catalogues. In addition, of the

5797 vegetable varieties appearing in commercial seed catalogues, 3002 are offered by only one company, with another 883
offered by only two companies. In other words, unless strenuous
efforts are made to save these seeds, there could be a tremendous
loss of genetic diversity in just this area of vegetable seeds in the
next few years.[49]

> There is a region in India that today has no food, because a tribal
> group that lived off forests, on forest herbs and forest tubers and
> forest produce, who 20 years ago were living on 180 varieties of
> food from the forest, were called primitive. So you introduced the
> Green Revolution to teach them rice farming and what you have
> at the end is collapsed rice farming because it was not ecologically
> sound, and you have deforested the region and produced famine
> where there had been none.[50]
>
> ---
>
> North and South, the value of diversity in agriculture is that it
> reduces risk; for the vast majority of farmers around the world
> that is far more important than maximising productivity. Farm-
> ers use diversity to forestall calamity.[51]

UNIFORMITY

Monoculture – the deliberate choice of uniformity and the continuous production of a single crop – appears to be a prerequisite
to industrial agriculture. For example, machine harvesting requires that every plant or fruit or vegetable in a field be ready for
harvesting at one time and by a single process. There is no way
of harvesting what is ripe and leaving the rest for a later round.
Three kinds of uniformity are thus demanded of every field: a
single crop; uniformity in maturity; and, uniformity in size and
shape. Since this is quite unnatural, various agro-toxins often
have to be used to achieve the required uniformity, such as top-
killers and growth regulators, in addition to the breeding, engineering, or selection of the seed for uniformity. Hybrids are attractive because they provide this uniformity along with other
attributes. A recent addition to this arsenal of weapons is the
broad-spectrum herbicide glyphosate (Monsanto's Roundup)

which is now licensed for use as a pre-harvest desiccant on canola, barley, and other crops. The maltsters, however, say they will not accept barley treated this way because the brewers won't use it!

> Sudanese farmers plant three crops in one hole; sorghum towers above sesame, while water melons creep along the ground.[52]
>
> ---
>
> Native Canadian storyteller Lenore Keeshig-Tobias describes the Three Sisters of traditional aboriginal agriculture as corn, beans and squash: the squash covers the ground as a living mulch, while the corn is a living pole for the beans.

The demand for uniformity prohibits cultural practices like intercropping – the growing of complementary crops in the same field – as well as the spreading of the harvest season so that it is less intensive and thus less demanding on both machinery and labour. Potato production is a good example. Until the harvester was introduced around 1965, thirty acres was about the maximum size of a New Brunswick potato farm. The family could perform the regular seasonal work while relying on additional local labour, school children and others, for the harvest. The schools accommodated this in their scheduling. The harvester, however, required a minimum of eighty acres of potatoes to finance the machine. This increase in farm size in turn required a whole new system of machinery since the family could no longer perform the regular work required to grow that large a crop. This transformation of New Brunswick (and Prince Edward Island) farming brought with it farm closures and farm consolidation as well as a drastic increase in farm capitalization. The social and ecological consequences were equally drastic.[53]

While uniformity in the field is required by the machine that will harvest it, the size of the field is strongly determined by the size of the machine. The size of the machine is, in turn, determined both by the functions assigned to it and by the economics of producing the machine. A sugar combine or a potato harvester must be big machines because of what they are required to do, and the fields must be of a certain minimum size to permit even the turning of the machine, to say nothing of its efficient operation.

Mechanized seeding, watering, cultivating, and fertilization also impose their requirements on the production process, but the requirements for uniformity do not end with the harvesting of the raw material. The processing itself requires uniformity, as does the packaging and even the transporting of food.

For example, while the McIntosh apple has been the most popular apple in Ontario for growers and the public since early this century, the Empire is gaining fast. Whether this is because the public prefers it to the Mac may be open to some question. Produce managers want a '12-month' apple that can survive long storage and rough handling. The Mac, discovered by John McIntosh in 1811 as a wild tree and subsequently bred for flavour and keeping qualities into the apple we know so well, is being overtaken by an apple developed by scientists at the New York State Experimental Farm in Geneva, N.Y. in 1966. An apple industry executive commented that the industry needs a "hardware-type product" like the Empire in order "to withstand the rigors of today's modern packaging and merchandising techniques".

We encountered the industrial demand for uniformity on our own farm when we tried to seed bromegrass and alfalfa together. (They are excellent companion crops because the alfalfa fixes nitrogen in the ground which the bromegrass utilizes, and they have similar growth patterns.) But bromegrass is a large, light, chaffy seed, while alfalfa is a small, round, heavy seed. It is virtually impossible to seed the two simultaneously except with a piece of expensive, specialized equipment. The alternative is to make two passes over the field. So even though the two are particularly suited as companion crops, the farmer is tempted to settle for some other mixture that can be seeded in one pass for the sake of immediate efficiency or productivity, meaning how much can be done by one person in the shortest possible time. This does not encourage either genetic or practical diversity.

Mechanical uniformity is only one expression of the uniformity sought and demanded in the food system. One established means of achieving uniformity, and greatly increasing the distance in the food system, is through hybridization. This is a process of selective breeding through traditional practices, or now through genetic manipulation, that produces a plant, or even an animal as in the case of a mule (a cross between a horse and a donkey), that is incapable of breeding true, or in some cases, breeding at all. Seedless mandarin oranges, the hundreds of corn hybrids (Ontario farmers alone can choose between more than 260 hybrid varieties), many ornamental plants and flowers, as well as strawberry plants all share this common character with mules: they are evolutionary misfits, incapable of reproducing themselves. In so far as we build our food system upon them, our food system is similarly dependent on the designers, inventors, and technicians who reproduce these plants and animals, and the corporations that employ them.

It is worth noting, in passing, that like many aspects of industrial agriculture that are considered 'conventional', hybridization as it is practised today is a very recent phenomenon. The first commercial crop of hybrid corn was not grown in the U.S. until 1920. Traditionally, the word hybrid was used to describe a simple cross of two lines of the same species (what we would today refer to as simply 'cross-bred'.) What hybridization came to mean, based on the work done in corn starting in about 1910, was the crossing of two 'inbred' lines, or two lines that had been bred back to themselves until they were considered pure lines with their natural variations bred out of them.[54] While this process, at least in corn, creates a peculiar first generation vigour known as heterosis, the kernels thus produced cannot be used as seed because their genetics break down when reproduced. They fall apart and do not breed true. This is not true of traditional crosses. The consequence, and a crucial factor in the development of industrial agriculture, is that the farmer has to go back to the breeder to purchase new seed every year. The farmer's autonomy and self-reliance are abolished by this relative simple process of inserting the corporate agenda into the genetic makeup of the seed.

Hybridization produces uniformity with a vengeance, as well as being "the prime mover for the industrial appropriation of the natural production process".[55] Current work underway by virtually every major seed company (all six of them) in the hybridization of canola (modified rapeseed) stands as testimony to the power of the corn model, whether practical in another species or not. The counterpoint, as you might expect, is the total neglect of open-pollinated varieties, except as stepping stones to hybridization. Open-pollinated varieties, of course, allow the farmer to save the best seed and plant it next year. In this process the farmer is also selecting the seed that has done best under the particular conditions of that farm, and thus the natural diversity of the crop is being increased, not decreased. It is the inbreeding that deliberately narrows the genetic bases and casts off all unwanted genetic material.

So global agribusiness, from Cargill to Continental, from ICI to Pioneer Hi-Bred, from Monsanto to Ciba-Geigy, with biotechnology and traditional plant and animal breeding, is creating proprietary (privately owned and probably patented) totally uniform living machines for the production of food as well as non-food commodities as the raw material for the processing industries. The result is the *trivializing* of agriculture,[56] the transformation of agriculture into a manufacturer and supplier of component parts for the transnational food assembly corporations. Fast approaching is the day when our food will be assembled much like a 'world-class' automobile with the components, or parts, being 'sourced' from whatever supplier will produce them most cheaply, anywhere in the world. The sources may be low-wage growing areas, states with minimum ecological protection legislation and enforcement, or protein or starch factories located next to the major markets for food products.[57]

CHAPTER 6

STORIES FROM THE LAND

While Cathleen and I were farming we started publishing *The Ram's Horn* as a newsletter for sheep farmers. It gradually broadened in scope and readership. Over the years we have published some stories from other farmers as well as our own. These are a few of them, the "photo album" for this book.

ON BLUEBERRY HILL

JOHN MILDON
Upper Stewiacke, Nova Scotia

Every year, about this time, the notices go up in our local Co-Op inviting the young people of the community to sign up to rake blueberries. During the dog days of August, it is the last ritual of summer before the school year begins again.

Throughout the province, the scramble will be on to harvest Nova Scotia's richest export fruit. Mobs of kids in sneakers, bright coloured T-shirts and jeans will bend over in the hot sun, rake in hand, and straggle out along lines of string on the barrens to gather the berries which contributed $16 million to the economy last year.

If progress has its way these same kids will soon be kicking stones on street corners along with all the other students who have vainly looked for work to help pay their school bills, or augment their pocket money. This year, for the first time, 22 mechanical harvesters constructed by Bragg Lumber in Collingwood will be operating throughout the province. If they work as well as expected, there will be more and eventually hand raking will be a thing of the past.

There are those who will argue that is good. To force youngsters to work in the heat and race to fill their buckets for minimal wages is exploitation of labour at its worst. Many growers will be relieved. Young labour is a headache: crews to be organized, picked up, taken home, paid. Some of them goof off, trample more than they rake, distract their friends, fall sick, or want the bathroom. Machines are far better.

Or, you can look at it this way: blueberries are a useful little cash crop for many farmers. The harvest is almost a family affair. The kids are mostly their own, or their neighbours'. The youngsters know each other. Most of them want to rake willingly and with enthusiasm. It is a sport as much as a job. It is a challenge, a contest of stamina, speed, dexterity. Boys and girls vie with their best friends. The girls try to outstrip the boys in adolescent, asexual competition. At the end of it, the dollars in the pocket reflect accomplishment, encourage independence and self-reliance.

The mechanical harvester will change that. Smaller growers will not be able to afford the capital investment. They will continue to hand rake until it is no longer competitive. Then their best acreages will be sold off or leased to someone with a machine. The marginal land will revert to bush. Machines, unlike kids, can only harvest the larger, more open and flatter fields.

The use of herbicides to kill competition, and fertilizer to increase yields, will increase to make the machine more cost-effective.

A larger share of the grower's dollar will be spent on materials and machinery from outside the community.

The kids will put their energy into defacing the post office, or kicking in the windows of the gas station and store.

It's a shame about the blueberry festival. That string of Bragg harvesters proceeding through the village is not as pretty a sight as the parade of floats done up by the growers and their picking crews that we used to see hereabouts.

And you can't blame the womenfolk for serving up those Mc-Cain's frozen blueberry pies, but do you remember those plates of fresh homemade blueberry muffins, grunt, tarts, and the jams and preserves?

I'm not against progress. It's against me.

from *The Ram's Horn*, August 1984

FARMERS AS EXPLOITERS

from a conversation with
DARRELL McLAUGHLIN
Aroostook, New Brunswick

On the other hand, we need to also be aware of farmers as exploiters. The desperation to maintain the 'lifestyle', the tradition, the family heritage, results in exploitation of: first, the wife, through overwork and isolation; then, the children, with the statement that they will receive just what the rest of the family receives (that is, food and lodging); and then of course the land and animals are exploited; and then the employees. I am aware of a tendency to pad my living at the expense of the people I employ: around me I see workers making up the difference between viable and non-viable farms; wage-labourers replace farmers; UIC and welfare payments replace subsidies to farmers. If you add up New Brunswick's total potato production and divide it by the man-hours of work of farmers and wage-labourers, you come up with the figure that at present, 60% of the potatoes produced in New Brunswick are produced by wage labour.

You have to remember that the Maritimes' tradition is rural; the people who settled here came themselves from a rural background. But at this time, with the change in society and the availability of work in town or country, it seems to me that the people who continue to live in the isolated rural areas are casualties, victims, or refugees of our advancing society.

Growth: if you go for a 50-100 hp tractor you have to farm your neighbour's land. And it is outside forces that are designing this technology; it is not coming from the farmers, who are poorly organized and therefore unable to describe their technological needs in a powerful way. One should also recognize that, for example, the 15-bottom plow takes *more*, not less, time, and requires more production. It's clear that the reason for this technology is not really to make life easier for the farmer, but to change the nature of farming. It has changed the inter-dependence of rural communities to raw dependency.

Without getting romantic about it, I think we can talk about the sense of satisfaction farmers get from working. There isn't anything quite like the feeling when after pushing yourselves harder than you thought you could, the job is finally done. In the potatoes area, when the potatoes are all in the potato house and you say to yourself, well, we did it. I think what has given life to farmers is producing. But now some farmers are working just to be consumers, whether it's bigger cars, tractors and trucks or CBs or whatever. I see a huge change from working to produce, to working to consume.

from *The Ram's Horn*, June, 1984

CROP FAILURE

BREWSTER and CATHLEEN KNEEN
Brookland, Pictou Co., Nova Scotia

It took a trip out West, listening to Prairie farmers talk about the drought and the threat of grasshoppers, to make us realize that as livestock farmers we also face crop failures. When it doesn't rain and the crop doesn't grow, that's clearly an 'act of God' about which we can do nothing but shrug our shoulders and, as farmers have for centuries, hope for a better year next year. That's what we usually think of as crop failure. In livestock it does sometimes happen too: when there's a freak storm in June and the newly-shorn sheep die of exposure, we can be philosophical about it; when the weather turns suddenly ugly while the ram is with the ewes in the fall, we know we can expect fewer lambs to be conceived for the spring. But when a bunch of feeder lambs are in the barn two months after they should have gone to market, we look at them and blame ourselves for our bad management.

We have been well indoctrinated: we are responsible for everything that happens on the farm; if we fail it is our management that is at fault, always. This is surely the most insidious consequence of our industrial agriculture mentality: everything is supposed to be under our control. Only when it comes to the weather are we allowed to refuse responsibility. And even then there is the nagging doubt: could we not have arranged some shelter for the sheep? Could we not have forseen that storm?

There are certainly clear instances of mismanagement causing crop failure, especially for arable farmers: using the wrong chemicals or the wrong dosage, failing to harvest at the right time, seeding too late, planting too close. But on second thought, is the line so clear between mismanagement and crop failure? Are the grasshoppers an act of God, or a judgement on monoculture? Is it wise for us to provide such an attractive spread for insects that have their rightful place in a more diverse world? We are told that the spruce budworm is only destructive when faced with a forest of uniform age and species, again an invitation to a certain insect to 'pig out' at our expense. Perhaps it is bad management to create conditions attractive to such 'acts of God'. When the rain failed last summer, it was reported that those farmers using the most chemical fertilizers were the hardest hit, because there was not enough moisture to make the fertilizer available to the plants; the organic farmers with healthier soil did not encounter such an extreme problem.

When the children used to complain and ask why they had to go out and do chores, we told them it was because we had a responsibility to the sheep. We had put them in a situation in which they could not fend for themselves, and so it was our duty to care for them. Our assumption was that we were in charge, in control. And when problems arose, we tore our hair and spent substantial amounts of time and money trying to correct our deficiencies as managers. It has been only recently that we have begun to wonder if some of our 'failures' are not inherent in the system itself.

This fall, we found our feeder lambs losing weight instead of gaining. A number of them died; others eventually began to recover but were losing their wool. (When sheep are ill, particularly with a fever, the wool stops growing. When they recover and start growing wool again, there is a break in the fleece and often the old wool just falls off.) We took dead and dying lambs to the pathology lab, but they could find no common cause. What were we supposed to think? We finally narrowed the cause down to the barley we were feeding: it seemed to be the only variable. Of course, by the time we realized what was happening it was too late, we were on another batch of barley. We are told that the chemicals used here or there in feed production – herbicides, pesticides, fungicides – are all safe as rain, but was the barley toxic? Was the fault in our management?

It is precisely our high level of management skills which leads us to specialize, in this case to work with age- and breed-specific groups. Good management demands that as many of the sheep as possible lamb at the same time so that they can be handled as a group. Now we wonder if many of the disease problems are not directly related to having a large number of animals so similar in age and susceptibility together under such intensive management. The point is, this strategy of developing uniform groups of animals that can receive appropriate treatment *as a group* is essential if the two of us are to be capable of keeping enough sheep to earn anything approaching a living wage from them. It is, in fact, essential to good management under an industrial system of agriculture.

Must we, then, assume individual responsibility for these 'crop failures'? Or are they an inherent part of that same skilled management which imposes such requirements on the wiles of nature? Would it be reasonable to suggest that crop failures, for the livestock farmer and for the arable farmer, are in part due to the fact that we are no longer one and the same?

Perhaps we should interpret crop failures in an entirely different manner: not as a failure to manage skillfully or diligently enough, not as our failure to have done enough research or applied enough technology, but as a judgement on our management system itself and, even more importantly, on the notion that we can or even should manage everything according to our very limited insights and understanding of the world we live in.

from *The Ram's Horn*, April 1985

SOME THOUGHTS WHILE FALL PLOWING

AL SLATER
St. Mary's, Ontario

October is the plowing month. It's a time when the tractor is on 'automatic pilot' with its front wheel stuck in the furrow. Watching the rich black soil turning in three ribbons behind the plow promotes a lot of thinking.

The land I am plowing has been in hay or pasture for three years straight. This means that in the whole three years the land has not been plowed or re-seeded. It has not been bare at any time so no wind or water erosion has occurred. The land being turned over is full of roots and worms: a healthy state of affairs. We try to run a *low-entropy* farm. We are labour intensive. Our cows go to pasture in the summer and we feed them hay and grain in the winter. Most of our land is covered in grass and hay so we don't have erosion problems. With this kind of crop rotation we need no pesticides and not a great deal of fertilizer. Our energy requirements are low because our machinery is small and old to match the small amount of crop we grow each year.

I come to the end of the field just as the ring-billed gulls fly in to feast on the worms. They are beautiful birds, vibrant, raucous as they glide down with heads turning to search the ground for worms. But we cannot allow all our worms to be systematically eaten by these hordes. So I reach for the .22 sitting on the tractor. I take a couple of shots to scare the birds off. They all lift off then circle and land again. Sadly, I accept my next task. I draw bead on an unfortunate gull and pull the trigger. Thousands of gulls rise and leave for an hour or so. But one takes a couple of steps then flops on the ground. I run over to break its neck so it won't suffer. Its body lies there, a cool wind blowing its feathers, serving as a warning to gulls not to land. The body haunts me as I travel round and round the field. I hate shooting birds.

But why am I plowing during the day like this? Most years I simply plow at night when the gulls are not feeding. But this is the year that I have to accept the reality of the market. Con-

sumers are using less beef and dairy products. Some, like ourselves, have cut back a little on meat for health reasons. Others,
including some of our friends, are starting to see vegetarianism
as some sort of moral statement. For us on this dairy farm it
means that we have made a substantial cut in our cow herd. More
land has to be plowed and planted to something vegetarians will
buy and eat. They don't eat hay and pasture so our rotation won't
be quite as good. There will be less roots and worms in our plowed
ground in a few years. Our land won't get as much manure as it
has in the past. If things get much worse we will be back to using
chemical weed control because our choices of crop rotations to
kill weeds will be severely limited.

I don't want to complain about soybean growers or people
who use them. Soybeans are an important food crop. But the
crop worries me. In Asia soybeans are grown using labour intensive methods. In the rest of the world soybeans have become a
'high-tech' crop. In Third World countries like Brazil land has
been taken from the peasants for multinational companies who
grow soybeans for export while local populations remain malnourished. Here in Ontario land planted to soybeans remains
bare in the spring until early June. Soil is subject to wind and
water erosion for a long time. I suspect that a good deal of organic
matter is oxidized by the sun during the long days at that time of
year. Beans seem to like a fine seed bed and they grow close to
the ground so the land has to be carefully levelled at planting
time for proper harvesting. By the time the beans are planted
the soil is worked so fine that very little structure remains. After
harvest the land is black again because the bean straw provides
very little coverage. Some bean stubble gets planted to winter
wheat but the rest lays black and vulnerable all winter. I really
hope I don't have to start growing soybeans.

As I start down another long furrow I am left with a lot of
questions. Will my soil ever be as good again now I am forced to
cut back on hay and pasture in the rotation? Will there ever be
as many worms again? How much new machinery will be needed
to match the increase in crop acreage? How will it be paid for?
And how much more fuel will be used? Will people around the
world be better fed as we switch from animal production to grain

and soybean production? Is there not already a glut of beans and grain while people are starving?

I look up from the tractor wheel rolling down the furrow. There in the middle of the farm are the two oaks standing side by side. They first put their roots into the soil 130 years ago when my great-grandparents first came here. Over in the pasture are the cows. Their ancestry reaches back to that time on this farm too.

Some people are vegetarians who reject animal products. Some people are bankers who reject us as inefficient. Some people are polluters who send acid rain and fouled air over our land. Are these people rootless?

from *The Ram's Horn*, Dec. 1985

ON BEING A SOJOURNER

BREWSTER KNEEN
Brookland, Pictou Co., Nova Scotia

A few evenings ago I went for a walk at dusk, checking the sheep and viewing the farm from the hill across the brook. I was moved to tears by the quiet, the beauty, and the pathos. The sheep, once I spoke, recognized me and paid no attention, except for those nearest who looked up. I realized that they had all been born and raised here; they know the farm better than I do, in a way.

The pathos accompanied the realization that even after 14 years here I know so little of this place, this land and its life. I am only a sojourner, a transient, here (like the sheep) only briefly; but unlike them, in that brief time I presume to take charge and to order this territory the way I want to. The old stone fences in the woods remind me of how rapidly the mark I have made can fade. I guess I've never really become a modern farmer: I've been a little too ambiguous to achieve that sense of certainty that seems to be essential to industrial, technological, capitalist production.

Sojourner is an interesting word: it means someone who is on the move, but who has stopped for a while. If farmers everywhere regarded themselves simply as sojourners, would we lose that sense of mastery and become more gentle and accommodating?

Yet there is a contradiction, for the farmer must also put down roots, be committed; it is as much a question of being owned by the land as of owning it. Does this mean staying put? Or might it mean being part of a community (it was once a family) that stays put for generations and puts down roots? What farming needs is a commitment to a place, without domination. Others will come after us, and what is left for them is up to us.

Sojourner is a Biblical word, and there is an analogy here with the Christian life, and the Biblical notion of the people of God. Sure, it is difficult to live with all the contradictions, but that is what faith is all about. Our culture runs into problems of stewardship – and good agriculture – when we want to eliminate risk, when we try with all our might to determine the consequences of all that we do by gaining (so we think) ever greater control over every step of the process. This is what leads us into our dependence on agrotoxins of all sorts, into our practices of monoculture, into our pursuit of uniformity, into factory farming.

Surely it is the delicate balance of the sojourner, between the need for roots and the need to move on, that is worth the seeking.

from *The Ram's Horn*, September 1985

A LETTER HOME

REBECCA KNEEN

enroute to Vancouver, B.C.

Dear Parents:

At the moment my perceptions of the farm crisis are somewhat obscured from the grit in my eyes from my first real Western brownout (a dust storm, not electricity at half power as I always thought). There wasn't a lot of drifting, just clouds upon clouds of filmy dust whipped off any bare field by 80 kph winds. It suddenly made me realize what 'dryland farming' really means. It's a lot more than being able to grow all those cereal and oil-seed crops, more than rationing household water use. Seeing your land get picked up and blown away in one storm, then watching your granaries or house get torn up in another really changes your understanding of your relationship to the land.

It is also difficult to write about the slow death that is the farm crisis in the face of the events at Oka. Now that Natives have reached the boiling point over their land, it is more than ever obvious that their natural allies are farmers. The fury, the need to take drastic action to save their people, their culture, and their land which drives the Native rebellion are all exactly the same feelings as those which have motivated farm-gate protests across the West.

Whites seem to feel they are being held hostage by Indians, [but] what would happen if farmers, too, began blocking roads? We can no longer hold to the dangerous vision of a society split, neatly, in half, between French and English, rural and urban, or rich and poor. Canada's self-acclaimed 'cultural mosaic' has come, somewhat, to pass: we have created a society not of two solitudes, but of many.

Here on the Prairies, distance, individualism, and an increasing and unrecognized poverty combine to provide an atmosphere of stifling isolation. The unspoken dictum of self-reliance cuts farmers off from their natural allies, the Native people. Both farmers and Natives have suffered from government policies designed to depopulate their communities, policies which sacrifice rural life and local sustainability to the interests of the urban upper class. Both have had their distinct cultures ignored and destroyed by the economically dominant culture. Both suffer from severe economic and political deprivation in a society which does not value their lives, and suffer from the myriad social diseases of the oppressed, including addiction to drugs, alcohol, and violence. Both farmers and Native peoples face the loss of their land, and with it, their livelihoods, history and identity. For both, the solutions are the same: a drastic change in the power structure and values of society.

The Prairie pattern is of large, square farms separated by dying communities. Travelling across the Prairies is like travelling through a bizarre desert of wheat, with occasional oases of living families. To speak to farmers is all too often to speak to shell-shocked survivors of a bitter economic battle. Three out of five farmers in the Southwest corner of Manitoba are undergoing Farm Debt Review – which usually leads to foreclosure.

The stress of the farm crisis is very visible in its effect on the youth. The activities which are now popular among teenagers seem to alternate between a holier-than-thou rejection of rebellious acts and a total commitment to self-destruction – often in the same person. The same alcoholism and violence which permeates rural adult culture takes on a more desperate edge with young people. Teenagers in rural areas are doubly disempowered: they are part of their parents' perceived helplessness in the farm crisis, and they are devalued as 'immature' by the adult population. By their own testimony, no-one talks to them. The farm crisis rivals sex education on the list of taboo subjects. Neither parents nor teachers will ask youths their opinions or fill them in on the situation, the first because they are often struggling so hard to control their own emotions that they cannot cope with the more volatile reactions of teenagers, the second because there is an unwritten law about becoming too 'personal'.

Seeing the incredible stress their parents are under, watching the swift disintegration of the family and community, they see no future in the only way of life they know. Their parents often actively discourage them from farming. Added to this are the external pressure of television and movies which glamorize urban life beyond any link with reality. As kids move away from the farm, the population of rural communities ages; with a geriatric population, kids find little or no rural culture they can relate to. Like everywhere else, rural youth are pushed into temporary self-destructive rebellion, unsupported by any genuine analysis. Without analysis, there is little chance of this rebellion turning into long-term resistance and change.

from *The Ram's Horn*, September 1990

THE STORY OF FARMER DAN

DAN WIENS
St. Adolphe, Manitoba

Commercial raspberry grower Dan Wiens and his wife Wilma farm on the southeast side of Winnipeg. In 1992 they began farming for 200 families in a Community Shared Agriculture project. In the fall of 1992 Dan described what had happened and I transcribed some of his remarks:

Last year at this time we had an idea. We called a meeting of city people and farmers to see what we could do together. We wanted to create a direct link, so that when the consumer pays a dollar the farmer gets a dollar. We wanted to create a system where there is dialogue, where we could find out what makes us tick, city people and farmers.

Policy and money decisions are made in the city, and the city doesn't have a clue about what is happening in the country.

We had a few meetings, and then we heard about CSA – Community Shared Agriculture, not Community Supported Agriculture as it has been called. I would be the farmer.

We set a limit of 200 families who could have shares in our farm, who could actually have a farm by buying a share in the crop. People have teachers, doctors, lawyers . . . now they could have a farmer, so I become their family farmer.

We got some good publicity in the Winnipeg paper and within a day and a half we had over three hundred phone calls. Virtually all those people had their cheque books open. They had it in their mind that this was a way they could do something positive.

We said, in effect, you don't have to be frustrated with this megasystem that's draining the lifeblood out of our rural areas and out of the province. We can short circuit the system.

We did not offer them cheap food. We said cheap food is killing us. Our children and grandchildren are going to pay for it.

So we gathered people in geographic groups around the city. The churches were getting in touch with us because they saw this as a way of becoming more socially relevant, so we took their parking lots as depot sites for geographic areas – not communities, because they are not that.

We called people together, and told them they had an opportunity to share the risk of farming. We told them that the large group of 200 families were going to share the farmer's risk. It was about food as close to the cost of production as possible. I see this as the way to agronomic sustainability and side by side with it a model of economic sustainability. By eliminating all the middle people, the consumer may pay just a bit more, but the farmer gets a fair return. Lowest possible price is not the objective. No longer are market forces the bottom line.

I was socialized like everyone else to see profit as the bottom line, I have to confess that. But why can't we have a system where everyone wins? The farm family wins because they have a wonderful lifestyle, they get a retail price for their food, a bunch of friends, and a guaranteed market and income. The consumers win because they start to feel a part of some sort of community, they feel like they are doing something decent, they get wonderful fresh vegetables, they get to know the person that is growing them, and they get some understanding of how food is produced and the ebb and flow of life.

Children loved it. They called me Farmer Dan. I have the hope that in a generation from now there will be children who know farmers and know that they have a farmer out there.

We had people helping, volunteering their labour.

We started a waiting list. We had meetings and asked people how they wanted their food delivered. They had a part in that.

We didn't give the people what they wanted, we gave them what the land provided. They had to order their diets not around what they wanted, but around what nature provided. At the end of the summer a lot of people came to me and said, it felt so good, being even a little bit in touch with nature.

We had a nutritionist on our volunteer staff, and a weekly newsletter describing what the people were getting and what could be done with it, and the nutritionist talked about the value of eating food in season and even fresh the same day because it is actually still alive ... People said they felt better, and some of the men said they were skinnier – they may have been romanticizing a bit ...

At the end of the year we had 200 happy people.

We had too much sweet corn, and people began giving it to their neighbours, and now these neighbours all want to get involved. We also offered beef and chickens and other things like eggs from adjunct farmers. We are creating new farms on the prairies ...

If just 20% of the population of Winnipeg were to purchase food for 14 weeks – the rest of the time Safeway's got them – if they were to purchase their vegetables, poultry, eggs and other things through a direct marketing scheme or shared farming, that would create 1000 farms! This is not replacing any farms, it is just utilizing available land.

When you go into Safeway and buy cabbage for ten cents a pound you don't see the farmer, and if you can get it for eight cents, you buy it. In our case, when the people know you and they see our cabbage for ten cents a pound, and they have experienced what it is like to weed cabbage, they say, forget it, I'm not going to pay you ten cents, I'm going to pay you 20 cents. That is exactly what has happened. We are adding culture to agriculture. We're putting some humanity back in it.

Food was delivered in blue boxes. People took them home and next week brought back their compostable material – the husks and cobs from sweet corn, for example. It's a low energy system, a much tighter system.

If people got something they did not want, they could put it in the community basket at the depot. People on holidays did not have to worry about their vegetables because their week's vegetables would also go into the community box to be delivered to a family in need – always tactfully done – or to the food bank. People felt good about that because they knew it was going where it was needed.

The city people came from every situation. Single mothers

and doctors and everyone else. A number of people came to us and said, We have no money. With all the community spirit behind this, we did not say no. We gave them a share because with all the community spirit behind this, it wasn't really going to hurt me. And then they wanted to work, so they volunteered their labour. Then a few big commercial farms bought some shares to give to the people who could not afford them. So even people fully in the system recognized this and wanted to make it work.

from *The Rams Horn,* December 1992

CHAPTER 7

THE FAMILY FARM
AND THE RURAL CRISIS

Farmers are now 2% of the population in both the U.S. and Canada. There are about 255,000 *census* farms in Canada. The bottom one-third of these farms receive 4% of the country's total farm revenue, while the top one-third receive 79% of the total farm revenue. This leaves the middle third with 17% of the farm revenue.[58]

We all heard about the 'farm crisis' for most of the 80s, or experienced it directly and painfully. If we don't hear so much about a crisis now, it is likely because the media story is an old one, on the one hand, and because a lot of farmers have resigned themselves to what appears to be the new reality of 'global competition'. There is little talk of cycles, or of things getting better next year, and a lot of farmers who have not settled with being 'businessmen' have had to find other work. But the crisis of industrial agriculture, and the crisis it has forced on rural communities, has not gone away. Nothing has changed that might make it go away. On the contrary, without radical change, one can only expect it to get worse.

As farm numbers continue to shrink while the remaining farms get larger and larger, the economic and social infrastructure consolidates and centralizes, the towns wither, and people get used to driving 50 or 100 kilometres to do their shopping at the malls and superstores. Federal policy, of course, intended this all along, in the name of modernization, progress, efficiency

– and corporate desire. Now, into the 90s, neo-liberal determinism and the reactionary campaign preaching the evils of debt have done their work. The crisis of farm and rural community pale before the trumped-up disaster of debt.

But not everyone has forgotten their roots, and the inability of the cities to cope with the disparities of wealth and the consequent social problems seems to be reminding urban residents that there might be another world out there. There once was, we remember.

There is a lot of sanctity and sentiment surrounding 'the family farm', and some of it was well-used to elicit public support before the media tired of the issue. But like the new realism that recognizes the fragile, often violent condition of marriage and the family, we should also be realistic about the structure and social relations of the family farm.

There are significant values and experiences that are implied in the concept of the family farm. The physical labour in which every member of the family took part is not an experience urban dwellers can easily imagine. The self-reliance of farm and community, living close to nature, the experience of the seasons and the power and wonder of life forces, whether expressed in the early spring racket of the peepers, the troublesome mounds of the ground hogs, the sprouts pushing their way above ground or the bleat of a lamb or the moan of a calf as it gets a hold on life, are all experiences beyond the urban realm. While reviewing family photographs of early days on the farm, we had to laugh when we realized that practically every picture of our daughter as a child had her holding a baby lamb, a chicken, a cat, or even the bull! Never a Barbie doll or even a toy truck.

One of the problems with the imagery and language is that it always refers to *the* family farm, or simply to farmers, as if there were a generic farm or farmer, all virtually identical, like no-name peas and ice cream. The images are often like those of the framed cross-stitching hanging in the dining room. But our experiences have not been uniform, nor have they been uniformly positive.

There is no single class of farmers any more than there is a standard farm family. Shared characteristics and problems and hopes, probably, but some farms are cold industrial businesses while others are 'inefficient' human communities. Some farm families involve every family member in making farm decisions, while others adhere to the dominant hierarchical (patriarchal) patterns of the larger society. Some farmers take pride in being 'businessmen' while others are more concerned with their stewardship of the land and the life of their community. Some farmers have taken every opportunity to expand, buying out their neighbours along the way, while others have stubbornly resisted the urgings of the bankers to borrow and expand. Some farm children are taught to represent themselves as model suburban kids, while others are shunned by their classmates because their clothes are hand-me-downs and because they do chores before school every morning and after school every afternoon. These same kids may well enjoy at the same time the psychological health of knowing they do significant work, just as they can enjoy their physical strength and abilities. But who off the farm appreciates these increasingly devalued skills?

Industry does not hold people in high regard. Neither does capitalism. Since the 1960s the official vision of industrial agriculture has included as much capital and as few people as possible. Business Week, a voice of capital, recently carried a table of "The Productivity Pacesetters". The definition of productivity is simple: "sales-per-employee".[59] The fewer people you need, the higher you rank.

The 1969 Federal Task Force Report, *Canadian Agriculture in the 70s*, drew up a model for agriculture in 1990 and summed it up in these words:

> There will be a substantial reduction in the number of commercial farms. Some will be family farms but all will be rationally managed, profit oriented businesses. Farm mergers and consolidation will result in much larger units, not primarily for increased production efficiency, but to structure units that are large enough to afford better management.[60]

In the succeeding 20-plus years, the pressure to define the farm and the farmer in this way have not relented. It is almost a wonder there are any other sorts left.

The Canadian Farm Credit Corporation, together with Statistics Canada, has illustrated, with numbers, the process of polarization – what the agricultural economists call 'rationalization' – that has been taking place in Canadian agriculture. One way it does this is by dividing all farms into one of three equal categories according to gross farm revenues. The use of the category 'farm revenue' indicates, without making it explicit, that gross farm sales constitute only a portion of farm revenue, the other portion of farm revenue being made up of subsidies, crop insurance, stabilization payments, etc. 'Off-farm income' is another category.

The one-third of the farms with low farm revenues had only 16.6% of the total assets, 8% of the total liabilities, 4% of the total farm revenue, and 47% of the total reported off-farm income. Those with medium revenues had 26% of the total assets, 21% of the total liabilities, 17% of the total farm revenue, and 31% of the off-farm income. The one-third with the highest revenues had 57% of the total farm assets, 71% of the total debts, 79% of the total farm revenue, and 22% of the total off-farm income.[61] Compared to 1988, these figures show a slow but steady trend to increasing polarization. Not a surprise.

The picture of the family farm painted by these figures is bad enough, but still does not convey the full truth that there is no direct correlation between gross farms sales and net farm income from sales. Among other factors, the farms with the biggest gross incomes owe the most money and are therefore paying the most interest. When added to the costs of other purchased inputs such as machinery, agro-toxins, seed, etc., and subtracted from sales, there may be little or nothing left for the family to live on.

It is also probable that there is a direct correlation between the debt, the gross sales, and the degree of industrialization of the farm. In plainer words, the best farmers, in terms of stewardship and community, may be those with the least debt, the lowest level of purchased inputs, and the least sales. They may also be living as well as or better than the high-velocity farmers.

Saskatchewan probably presents, today, the most stark picture of what is happening to North American industrial (production) agriculture. It is not yet normative, but it is probably prophetic. Saskatchewan is a farming province, though geography and climate confine it to production of small grains and livestock. What it mostly does is grow wheat, high quality wheat. The province reached its population peak sometime in the mid-80s, with a population of slightly more than a million according to the 1986 census, and it has been dropping since. Its number of farms peaked in the mid-1930s at about 143,000, with this figure steadily declining to 60,000 in 1991. Total farm cash receipts have remained steady at about $4 billion since 1981, meaning a steady decline in real income. While spring wheat acreage reached 18.5 million acres in 1966, it has basically ranged from 9 million to 17 million since 1918. In 1918 the farm size averaged about 360 acres, a half-section; in 1966 it averaged about 760 acres, and by 1991 it was slightly more than 1000 acres. The farm price of the wheat grown was $206/tonne in 1980, and it has not been near that before or since. In 1990 the figure was $115. And by 1993 the Farm Credit Corporation owned one out of every 47 acres cropped in the province as a result of farm foreclosures.

It's time we took apart the notion of the family farm, like the ultra-filtration of milk which we get to in Chapter 11, and separate it into its component parts to see what we are actually left with. Then we might want to make a social decision about what parts we want to relinquish, perhaps with a sigh of relief, what we want to keep and how we want to put them together. The alternative is to passively observe what is happening and accept it as inevitable. If we do this, then we ought, at least, to be aware that there are others involved in this 'inevitability' who are much less resigned or fatalistic.

The financial crisis in agriculture is not necessarily the same thing as the crisis of the family farm. Food production is now dominated by large commercial enterprises that may still be legally owned by a family, or a family owned corporation, but they are already too large to conform to any traditional understanding of family farm. On these farms, the primary role of the family is that of enterprise manager rather than the principal supplier of labour, and its large amount of capital may be controlled if not owned by external lending agencies. So while these farms may be nominally owned by the families working them, the role of their creditors (which often includes chemical and fertilizer companies) in their management, like the role of the World Bank and the IMF in the management of Third World debtor countries, may be greater than most would like to admit.

By contrast, the traditional family farm is an enterprise in which virtually all of the labour is supplied by members of the extended family, in which management is not separated from the labour itself, in which responsibility for decision-making may be shared among those doing the work, and in which capital requirements are small enough for the family to actually own the equity. It may be a farm that has been built up over more than one generation, in which the grandparents continue to have a role. Such a farm can be passed from generation to generation without the burden of debt, the grandparents being cared for out of the continued operation of the farm, rather than being pensioned off and shipped out, requiring cash withdrawal that depletes the farm operating resources. Very often, in this picture, there have been hired hands, but they functioned both structurally and socially more as uncles or children than as hired labourers. (In the context of a patriarchal society this has, of course, frequently been a very authoritarian structure, but it is not necessarily so.) With minimum cash flow and an extended family as the working unit, there was little opportunity for the wage differentials that alienate labour and management in industrial agriculture.

What has been valued in this model and is remembered is the integrity of the enterprise. Labour and management are not only non-adversarial, they are united in the same persons. Nor is capital treated as a separate aspect: it consists of the land which the family is working, which is not regarded as a marketable commodity; the limited machinery, which is basic and durable, again not to be bought and sold, but bought and repaired and used more or less forever; and livestock and stored feed or grain. Cash flow, which has become *the* criterion of capitalist enterprise, is marginal, though this is not to say that it is unessential. Within a form of self-reliant agricultural production, *minimal* cash flow is a sign of health, whereas in industrial agriculture the health of the enterprise is judged, by the banks, by how *big* the cash flow is. Thus news reports talk about gross farm income, which reveals absolutely nothing about the actual health of the farm or agriculture in general as I have already pointed out. The same thing can be said, of course, about evaluating a national economy by measuring its Gross National Product.

As a largely self-sufficient sheep farm, we had a rather low gross income, yet we knew that our net income, which is what we actually had to live on, was often greater than that of the hog farmer with ten times our gross income. The hog farm bought much of its feed and carried a large debt, and hence had a high cash flow, which we did not.

Our low gross income and low cash flow also reflected the labour intensity of our style of farming. We made deliberate choices about mechanization, and hence capitalization, based on acquiring machinery only to do what could not be done by hand, or by many hands. Thus we stacked bales on hay wagons by hand rather than investing in a baler with a bale thrower, costly steel wagons, and a bigger tractor to haul it all.

The largest number of farm units are still more or less traditional family farms, but they have always counted on off-farm employment, such as teaching, nursing, driving the school bus, fishing, or working in the woods for cash income. Mythology notwithstanding, the North American family farm has hardly ever been a viable enterprise in the sense of providing an adequate or complete income for the whole of the small community that lived on it. So it should not surprise us that today commodity prices, outside of supply managed dairy, eggs, and poultry, do not return enough to keep the family or the farm going.

The peak years for North American agriculture were 1978-79. Since then commodity prices have been falling steadily, while prices for everything else have been rising. This cost-price squeeze alone is enough to cause a very real crisis in agriculture, but the debt crisis facing large, capital-intensive industrial operations that expanded on a speculative market and are now caught short is something quite different and the two should not be confused.

The heart of the crisis, in fact, may not be farming as a way of life, or even commodity prices *per se*, but the ownership of the means of production: land, machinery and buildings (the visible signs of status and success). There is, after all, a substantial difference between farming as a vocation or a way of life, and farming as the ownership and management of capital. There is no inherent reason why a farmer must own the land he or she works. What is important is security of tenure.

Much of the farm crisis is due to the debt which was incurred when money was loaned and land purchased on the basis of the inflated and speculative land prices of the late 70s and early 80s. Like the fishing boats left high and dry in the Bay of Fundy at low tide, as land prices declined (about 50% since then) the farmers who bought at high tide are left stranded. In part it has been the farmers' own insistence that they have to own the land they farm which is now eliminating the farmers, but in part it was the banks who led them into it. Just as the banks made a lot of stupid and greedy loans to Third World countries, so they also made a lot of stupid and greedy loans to farmers. They did this because the banks make their money out of what used to be called usury, putting money out at interest. The banks, by their own logic, have to make loans, and as long as national governments will back them up and make amends for their greed and stupidity, the banks need not worry about the wisdom of their actions. (We return to this issue in Chapter 15.)

THE CRISIS IN RURAL COMMUNITY

So what is to become of rural Canada?

If there is a crisis in agriculture, increasingly it is being overshadowed by the crisis of rural community, or, more precisely, the destruction of rural community. What is mourned as farmers depart the land, as the government and its Market Economy agents dismantle the infrastructure of rail lines and schools and public services, is the possibility of community.

Rural Manitoba: we drove into the yard just in time to join a neighbourhood barbecue. It's not much of a farm community anymore since most of the neighbours work in town at one job or another. Not long ago 300 people or so lived there. The big grain elevator on the main line was at the centre of the town. The talk that evening was of how the elevator was going to be closed down. "Rationalization they call it."

Then the focus of the conversation shifted to the 'new' 3-bedroom house that had been built for the elevator manager not many years ago. The people we were visiting had moved three vacant houses already from the 'town' onto a single property so that they could enjoy some sort of community life. One of the men present was an assessor in a nearby town, and he said, "You wouldn't want to pay more than $8000 for the house alone. You would have to spend that much on a new foundation and then pay moving costs, and in town (25 km away) they can't give houses like that away for $25,000".

Rural Dignity sprang up in 1986 in one of Canada's remote corners when the Conservative government announced the rationalization of rural post offices, by which they meant another step in the dismantling of the infrastructure of rural society. Rural Dignity was a good name for a movement that understood that self-respect and identity are essential to any community. Take away the post office, the grain elevator, the feed mill, the bank, the farm machinery dealer – a town cannot survive with only the coffee shop and its gossip to hold it together.

When we moved to the farm in 1971 we had a ring-down battery powered telephone. The phone came with the farm and made us members of the Saltsprings Mutual Telephone Company. The switchboard was tended by Mrs. Roblee who was 82 when she retired. That was when we had to admit defeat and join Ma Bell. The first fall we were there, though, the line needed repair. Old Herbie had cut some trees off his farm for poles, and we hired a backhoe to dig the holes. It took about eight of us all of a Saturday to replace the poles that had rotted off and to put up the wires that had been laying on the ground, in some places for quite some time. But I met the neighbours as I would never have otherwise. The winter meetings of the phone company took place in Donald's kitchen, or in Isabel's – with 'lunch' afterward. Progress came to Saltsprings, and that same year we moved to Saltsprings the local school was closed. (The original district school half a mile up the road had been closed years earlier.) Our kids spent two hours a day – from age five – on Isabel's bus to get to a school that effectively took away another one of the reasons for there being a community in Saltsprings. Later the post office was moved down the road so it could be right on the highway, but not many could walk to it then. Progress and rationalization were not good for that community.

Who wants to live in near-total isolation without neigh-bours? The kids finish school, having clocked one lifetime al-ready in school-bus confinement, and move on. There is no longer a community for them, so what happens to the farm be-comes more a matter of nostalgia than choice. The crisis is social, but it is the result of the reduction of a society to nothing but a Market Economy.

Who will mend the social fabric when everyone is busy mak-ing money?

CHAPTER 8

ELECTRONIC FOOD

IT ONLY COUNTS IF IT MOVES – TECHNOLOGY AND CONTROL

As you go through the check-out counter of a large supermarket the clerk passes each item over a scanner. I'm always amazed that a laser beam (or beams) can pick up and 'read' the bar code so quickly. As the equipment has become more sophisticated, even unpackaged items like carrots, as long as they have a bar code on a label somewhere, are 'readable'. The carrots themselves will probably soon be genetically engineered so that each one contains its own bar-code: small adhesive brand labels are already appearing on fruit of all sorts. The latest news is that bar codes will soon be 'layered', or in effect three dimensional, allowing them to contain many times more information. The scanner, the bar-code on the label and the electronic price indicator on the shelf are the visible reminders of the fact that the computer both controls and makes possible the food system we take for granted.

The scanner, of course, is connected to an electronic cash register with a printer that can give you an itemized slip – or with an artificial voice that can tell you what you have purchased at what price! But this register is just the visible tip of the iceberg. The information entered into the computer at that terminal is not just the price of what you have purchased and the coupons you hand over. The cashier, if you are in a 7 Eleven store, might also be entering your sex and an estimate of your age so the managers, with Japanese efficiency, can find out who their best customers are and what they like to buy.

What is entered by the scanner is a precise list of everything that you have purchased, and this happens with each customer. In other words, every item that goes out of the store (paid for, that is) is immediately recorded as a debit to inventory in the main computer. Since everything coming into the store is likewise entered, the manager knows precisely, at all times, what is on hand. He (or she) knows what is moving and how fast (referred to in one trade magazine as "warehouse velocity"). The manager can also monitor the productivity of the clerks.

> Employees can now use cards that look like credit cards to check in and out. They can do one or more jobs a day at different rates of pay and, with the card, are paid for the work they do. If more hours are worked at a particular section than scheduled, the computer can tell who worked those extra hours and when. All the retailer has to do is find out why.[62]

The latest experiment is to let you scan your own groceries and turn the cashier into a kind of bank teller that you pay on your way out, utilizing your direct-debit bank card. This is, of course, one way to eliminate unionized labour, but it will probably require, in turn, a magnetic security tab on each item, like the higher priced clothing in Zellers.

> Point of Sale (P.O.S.) interface is presently being integrated across the chain to permit head office to automatically download information and price changes into P.O.S. scanning systems in all Sobey's stores. The P.O.S. interface will save time, improve store employee productivity, and reduce the potential for errors in pricing administration.[63]

There is a real efficiency in the system. Without electronic information processing to keep track of the 3000, 30,000, or 100,000 items stocked at any one time, this huge and highly centralized system would simply not be possible. Inventory control – knowing how much of what is where – is only the beginning. The computer can also tell the manager what is moving and what is not. Timely specials and discounts can keep the sluggards moving before they really back up and foul the system. (This has its good side in helping to reduce spoilage and waste.) If the retail outlet is owned/managed by the wholesaler/supplier, then the process can go back a step to include the warehouse. So the warehouse and the store are integrated, though spatially separated.

Some independents try to overcome this disadvantage by turning their stores into warehouses. Thus the 'warehouse store' with its goods stacked in cartons overhead or underfoot.

An interesting example is the collusion – the industry calls it 'partnering' – between Proctor & Gamble and Wal-Mart "to reduce costs and inefficiency through information sharing":

> P&G has access to Wal-Mart scanner data and has developed an automatic shipping system based on turnover information. The goal of the continuous replenishment system is to eliminate written orders and invoices.[64]

Such a system raises the interesting question of who is really in control.

There is yet another integrating step that can be taken. If the wholesaler is large enough, it can extend its control backwards not only to the supplier and manufacturer, but also to the processor. Again, information is the key. The processor may be owned by the wholesaler or may be operating under contract. Either way, the processor becomes simply one sector of transformation as the product moves continuously from the farm through the system and out the retail end. The processor/distributor can often pass this control on further back and specify to the grower or farmer what is to be provided, of what quality, and when, as we saw in Chapter 4. This results in contract farming where the buyer/processor may well specify the seed to be planted, the date it is to be planted, which herbicides, pesticides and fertilizers are to be used and when, and when and how the crop is to be harvested, often after some chemical has been applied to assure that the entire crop is ready for harvesting simultaneously on the day the harvester has been booked.

With both the U.S.A. and Canada planting 80% of their potato crops in only six varieties, the two countries are increasingly vulnerable to the threat of pestilence and fungal outbreaks which could devastate production just as severely as the Irish potato famine of the 1800s.[65]

The Canadian TNC McCain's, based in New Brunswick, is a good example of the intimate relationship that can develop between processor and farmer.

McCain's has chosen to work the area that includes farm input supplier, farmer, and processor, replicating its way of doing business in country after country. It controls the potato system from its position as major world processor, with 50 production facilities in nine countries and global sales of more than $3 billion, more than half of this from french fries alone. In 1992 McCain's processed more than 2.5 billion pounds of potatoes, selling the plain models for 26-32 cents (U.S.) a pound to restaurants, fast food outlets, and retailers.[66] Farmers in Canada in the 1992-3 crop year received 3-10 cents per pound from McCain's for their potatoes. The overall average price to farmers was in the range of 5-7 cents per pound; the cost of production is reckoned at 6-8 cents per pound.

Facilitation of this integration and centralization by means of electronic information processing – the computer – has not been confined to food processing and distribution. The farmer, or farm corporation, is also probably using a computer not only to keep financial and farm records, but to make day-to-day management decisions.

Innocently, the farmer may well be using computer software that is specially designed, and often generously supplied by, an input supplier like a feed company, to assist the farmer in utilizing all the latest advances in technology, like the transponder hanging on the cow's neck that is her personal key to an electronically controlled feeder which meters out feed according to her current milk production.

All the electronic gagetry required for this is yet another purchased input, and instead of the farm wife keeping the books – and the money – at home, the price of the computer and its software leaves the farm and the community.

If it is good management to gear up the cow and the farm in this way, it is certainly considered sound financial management to gear management of the farm not to soil and seasons, but to the commodities exchange, utilizing the computer again to speculate on the futures market – although this is more politely called 'hedging' – in order to 'stabilize' returns and increase 'profits'. But for this there is a fee as well, and, like the price of the computer, it too leaves the farm and the rural community, if not the country.

Computer software, like the computer itself and all other technology, is created by or within a particular time, location and culture. It is inevitable that it express an ideology, an organizing principle or logic, just as the plant expresses the characteristics bred into the genetic material of the seed. The designers and programmers of agricultural software, like their counterparts, the modern plant scientists, will express the ideology of their employers; and if they work for the agricultural establishment, whether government or corporate, their programs will more than likely express the Market ideology of productivity, efficiency, and competitiveness, along with the private ownership of the means of production.[67]

The majority of farmers are no more likely to be able to design their own computer programs for TMR (total mixed rations) than they are likely to have the capacity to design and build specialized equipment for field work, though they may know very well what they need. So the technology comes to define the choices.

Soon after we started farming, for example, I realized that I had two choices when faced with the tremendous number of stones in the fields. I could either try to pick them all off, or I could smash them back down into the ground. The latter seemed the more practical course, and through a British immigrant farmer I succeeded in importing a heavy Cambridge ridged-ring roller designed to do just that job. I never saw another such roller, though many farmers admired mine. The technology that was commercially available was rock picking machines. These are big and expensive and generally operated by contractors, but they are used because it is the technology that is available, even though a very small tractor could utilize my simple roller at much lower cost. This illustrates what I would call *technological determinism*.[68]

The seed the farmer plants may itself be the product of similar information processing. Working with the seed company, probably owned by one of the chemical companies supplying the life-supports required in the production process, the processor may be telling the university researcher (funded by the corporation) what characteristics are desirable. The researcher will then engineer the seed to meet those specifications using the same information processing technology to model the alternatives before actually creating them. As in the supermarket warehouse, electronic information processing provides the means to identify and select from the multitude of characteristics and combinations.

All that is needed to artfully explore the inordinate number of possible product combinations in the genetic, chemical, and microbial realms of agriculture is a computer.[69]

NutraSweet is looking at the next generation of high potency sweeteners and we're using computer modelling to do it. We know the size and shape of molecules common to sweetness and once we've isolated them in sweet-tasting products, we try to build molecules that resemble them.[70]

The seed finally winds up being merely an *envelope* for the package of genetic information created or assembled by the genetic engineer. Thus control over the production process passes back from the farmer to the designer of the seed itself, or rather to the company that provided the specifications the seed was to meet. The requirements and characteristics of the seed and what it produces will have been determined according to a particular economic ideology, and while the farmer and the processor may think they exercise some control over what they can do, their freedom is severely limited by what has been designed for them. This is another example of technological determinism: technology being developed and used by one interest or corporation to determine what others can and should do.

Yet we tend to regard technology as harmless or neutral. This book is being 'written' on a computer, so I am engaged in electronic information processing both externally and internally. Internally my brain and central nervous system are processing information via electrical impulses while externally the computer is doing the same thing, as an extension of my self since it is inert unless activated by me. In this sense it is just another piece of technology making human work easier, more fun, more demanding, or whatever. It all seems very harmless and the technology does invite collaborative work and information sharing (particularly via e-mail). It enables me to utilize information more extensively and with more facility than in pre-computer days.

But the technology I am utilizing has its own logic and Word-Perfect is the product of a particular culture. The computer I have chosen utilizes a zero-based (digital) system, and what I can do with it is limited by *its* logic; in other words, I have chosen to accept its limitations on my logic, even while I develop a critique of this logic. I have to operate within the limits as well as the logic of the technology I have chosen. This logic is also manifested in the relations of the production of the computer itself, with its component parts made in 'free trade zones' all over the world. And as Jerry Mander points out, it is a good idea to keep in mind who, and for what purposes, the technology was created in the first place: the military![71]

The diminishing gap between technology and its products, between the living and the inanimate, is aptly illustrated by the story of a 'virus' discovered in the fall of 1988 in a computer network in the U.S.A. *Science* magazine reported that, "The main computer network for researchers in the U.S. and overseas was disrupted for two days last week as managers tried to kill an electronic virus injected by a graduate student . . . The 60,000-machine system, some experts insist, was not infested by a true virus but by a relatively benign 'worm'. Unlike a virus, which breeds by insinuating its own logic into existing programs and making them bear its offspring, a worm remains self-contained. It lives off weaknesses in the host's logic. This particular worm did nothing but reproduce madly."[72]

This computer virus was not like a cancer virus that devours its host, though it could have been designed to do that. It was, however, self-replicating and had it gone unnoticed for a longer period might have done untold good in dismantling the military apparatus. Infecting the medical records of a large hospital, on the other hand, could be disastrous. There is an eerie similarity between the salmonella bacteria, or BSE, and the computer virus. So integrated are both food and computer systems that to get rid of the diseases it is almost necessary to shut down entire systems.

Access to and control over information may sound harmless, but what information you are provided with or have access to determines the context of your decisions. Equally, lack of information means lack of decisions and leads to passivity and powerlessness. This realization is fuelling new demands for more adequate information about what we are eating, as the U.S. Food and Drug Administration discovered in 1993 when they asked for public comment on proposals for food labelling in regards to biotechnology. There was so much public response, and it was so critical of the FDA's minimal, industry-dictated labelling proposals for the products of biotechnology, that the FDA had to reopen the period of public comment for another four months, an unprecedented step.

It appears that a growing number of people want not only to know what they are eating, but also where it comes from and how it is produced, starting with the seed. So we want to know first whether it is the product of genetic engineering or not, and if so, why? Then we want to know whether it is grown locally, and hence genuinely fresh and part of the local economy, or imported from a Third World country with underpaid labour. We also want to know how it is grown – agro-toxins or organic – and whether it has been treated with chemicals to help it survive the ordeal of travel and extend its shelf-life.

One of the more interesting information issues that troubles the biotechnology industry (corporate or university) is whether the *process* by which a product is produced should be publicly stated, as on the label, as well as what it is as a *product*. The biotech industry claims that how a product is produced does not matter as long as it is safe. But there are many people who want to know whether a food was produced by means of biotechnology or genetic engineering, such as milk from cows treated with recombinant Bovine Growth Hormone (BST) or tomatoes that have been genetically engineered for a longer shelf-life or canola oil made from canola plants genetically engineered to resist herbicides. This is before even mentioning the issue of transgenic foods and potential allergies!

In other words, people want more complex forms of information, and want enough information to be able to make an *in-*

formed as well as personally and socially *responsible* choice about what they eat. This is, after all, the one point at which everyone can cast a vote, as it were, for their economy of choice, regardless of official trade policies and corporate desires. All we need is reliable and adequate information – in the context of public policy that places human welfare and ecological responsibility ahead of capital accumulation.

The seed (or egg) is the carrier of genetic information as well as the means of production. The information it carries in its genes has to do not only with its internal characteristics, but also with the culture, the environment, it has come from and in which it may thrive. The term 'designer genes' is catchy, but it is also accurate. If the issue of control is significant, then we must look carefully at who the designers are and who they work for, just as we must in considering computer software design. In turn, we should consider whether we have any control over those corporate designers, and what social and moral criteria guide them in their decision-making.

The farmer who is not happy about accepting these corporate designs will soon find him or herself in a position very similar to that of the small genuinely independent retail grocer. Both count on a local or specialized market and are essentially operating speculatively; they have virtually no control over their selling prices. To the extent that they are labour intensive, they are unattractive targets of corporate takeover. It is precisely for these reasons that the dominant corporations increasingly encourage the independent operator, both as farmer and as retailer, as we have seen in Chapter 3. These so-called 'independents' (there are very few genuinely un-tied operators) create an impression of alternatives in the system and of opportunities for entrepreneurs. In addition, they provide a quality of service that no electronically controlled business dependent on turn-over and discounting can provide. The superstores pursue this logic to the extent of having independent operators within the superstores themselves, dealing in fresh fish or bulk foods, flowers or a deli, as pointed out earlier. These low-volume specialty shops or kiosks can increase the attractiveness of the entire store and increase the patronage, thus adding to, rather than subtracting from, the high-volume sales of the main store.

In the same way, there is a new interest in agricultural small-holders who will produce quality food, such as organic or 'natural' beef or vegetables, and specialized products such as goat cheese or wild-flower honey, products that the electronically controlled corporate or giant 'family' farms cannot. Nevertheless, when bulk food marketing was re-introduced a few years ago in health food stores, it was not long before the major chains followed suit. In the same way, the 'natural' or 'organic' categories are quickly captured by the capitalist marketing system and sidelined to the position of a high-profit niche product.

My son brought home a bag of chips and we tried them out: they are Hostess (owned by Kraft General Foods which is owned by Philip Morris – don't be fooled by the Canadian flag on the bag!) *Gibney's*, "Crispy Slow Cooked Homestyle Chips" tasting very much like the local, 'handmade' chips – *Miss Vickie's*, *Millie's*, and others – that hit the market as specialty products a few years ago as people began to seek healthier and more tasty food. The irony in all this is evident in the sell-out of Miss Vickie's to Pepsi/Hostess Frito Lay in 1993. The package does not indicate this, except in the locations of Miss Vickie's, which are all established Hostess plants. (In Chapters 14 and 15 we look more closely at organic and sustainable agriculture.)

The monolithic supermarkets of the 60s lost their public appeal rather quickly. The vulgar evidence of mere productivity could not hold an audience for long. In the same way, industrial agriculture lacks the appeal and charm of the family farm to the urbanite. In the sophisticated marketing of the food system of the 90s, it is imperative to develop the appearance of diversity and intimacy. The technology of electronic information processing has not only facilitated the centralization of the distribution system but also its apparent diversification and variety. Microbiology and genetic engineering would not be what they are without the computer, and neither would the Weston/Loblaws' empire.

CONTINUOUS FLOW

The poor tomato has become the butt of many a joke, the object of millions and millions of dollars of high-tech research, and the vehicle for a battle between corporate greed and public flavour. It gets designed in a laboratory and propagated in a corporate research facility by means of tissue culture before being set out in a greenhouse in California or in Holland. It grows some, and then is transplanted. It grows some more and bears fruit. No time to stand still. The fruit hardly notices the rough mechanical harvesting, designed as it has been with a tough skin. Maybe being designed is better than just being bred.

Then the tomato is packed and transported, like a charter vacation flight, pushed around a warehouse, transported some more, stacked and fondled and dumped in a cart just to be picked out again and weighed and rolled down a chute into yet another wagon, transported yet again and, mercifully, consumed shortly thereafter. Rather dizzying, all that constant movement. Hardly time to get your breath, much less to ripen.

Central to the logic of the food system controlled through electronic information processing is constant movement. The measure of productivity in this system is like water through a turbine, or the electricity meter in your home: it is the flow that counts. You are billed for electricity in terms of the flow of power. Volts is a measure of potential, amps is a measure of flow, and watts (volts x amps) is the measure of volume. You are charged for the number of watts consumed. Quantity is a function of movement.

But technology makes its demands. To be manageable electronically, the goods must be uniform – from seed to apple to cereal box. Every kiwifruit must be the same size in order to fit properly into the container that will be handled by electronically guided equipment into and out of the warehouse. The potatoes must all be close to the same size so they can be sliced according to an electronic formula for processing into chips in the most effective manner – after they have been mechanically harvested and graded and washed. Watch the cars going through an automatic car wash some time. The car is attached to an endless moving chain to go through the car wash, with maybe a little hand touch-up after it is detached. The potato or the milk or the chicken is little different. Processing tomatoes are literally floated out of the special steel trailers that haul them from the field onto the conveyor line for processing. They disappear into a building and the cans emerge at the far end already packed in cartons for shipping, with the labels of half a dozen different companies on them. The local farmers were forced to adopt the new technology – the trailer-mounted steel tanks – if they wanted to continue to grow and sell processing tomatoes. No more utility wagons hauling hay in June, basketsfull of tomatoes in August, and potatoes in October.

The consumer, too, must perform its function in this process. Its function is to consume, beginning at birth, preferably, with commercial infant formula. Advertising, packaging, and all the rest of marketing will provide all the help they can, but the product must *move* and if the customer will not buy it, the product must move anyway: to another store, to the sanitary landfill, to the food bank. That is why the big chains support the food banks which provide a socially acceptable dump or 'outlet' for the products that are not moving and defray, through tax write-offs, the costs of those that have to be dumped. As we saw in Chapter 1, since their emergence in the early 80s food banks have become sophisticated and integrated elements of the food system. Those who have been marginalized by being deprived of buying power are reintegrated by those willing to be surrogate customers on their behalf. Sales, cash flow, and the very health of the economy demand it.

The consumer responsibility to the food system is to buy and consume, to keep the product moving. If you function well you enable the stores to keep fresh product on the shelves, keep the stock clerks working on a uniform schedule, keep the stock moving through the warehouse – in one side and out the other – and keep the processing plant operating every day with a minimum of labour because it can be automated if uniform. The system will *source* its supplies wherever it can, regardless of politics or geography. Price, reliability and consistency are the only concerns. The raw materials will be processed wherever it suits the buyer, in most cases. That, in turn, will largely depend on labour conditions, and hence, politics, but wherever, it will all be made possible by modern communications technology.

Retail managers are encouraged to use software like *Spaceman* and *The Third Generation* to help them utilize their computers. *Spaceman* "ties floor planning, fixture engineering, market research, data processing, buying, merchandising and other related departments into a common merchandising operating environment. . . . Technology has altered the methods used to market and merchandise the front end (by the cash register) and it can help increase the profitability of an already profitable area."[73]

CHAPTER 9

FOOD AS INFORMATION

OWNING THE MEANS OF PRODUCTION

> Power is closely connected with the production of knowledge and
> with what is given the status of 'truth'.[74]

While it may seem far-fetched, there is no significant breach between the control of inventory in a modern food warehouse by
means of electronic information processing, the direct debiting of
your account at the check-out counter of the supermarket
through the same electronic information system, and the electronic manipulation and modelling of genetic information. If
your groceries can be kept track of by means of electronic information, so can your genes (and the entire human genome, the
complete human genetic code).

Electronic information processing has transformed the food
system before our very eyes, from the scanner at the check-out
counter to the university laboratory designing new saline-resistant wheat or producing synthetic growth hormone for pigs. But
the computer has become more than simply a means of managing
and controlling information, and even more than the means of
creating and controlling vast systems. It has actually become the
means of production, and this raises the question of ownership
and what are called Intellectual Property Rights.

Accumulation of capital – the theoretical essence of capitalism – is only possible on the basis of private property, that is, the

legal ability to exclude others from access to certain property which is the means of production. Thus Brazilian peasants are cleared like the trees off the land to make way for corporate soybean production, or landless peasants in the Philippines starve because they have neither employment on nor access to the land of the idle sugar estates, idle because of the lack of export markets for sugar. The reason why there has not been significant land reform in countries like the Philippines is obvious: there is a profound contradiction between uncontrolled private ownership of land and universal access to land as a means to production and survival.

There is a long history to these practices of depriving people of what they have viewed as common or public property. In the history of the West, we can, somewhat arbitrarily, go back to the Great Enclosure Act of 1845 in Britain that brought an end to the economy of the commons. (The enclosure movement had begun some 150 years earlier and 4000 Private Acts of Enclosure had privatized some 7 million acres of commons before the Great Enclosure Act was passed.)[75] Or we might refer to the repeal of the Corn Laws in 1846, which opened the door to the importation of cheap wheat from the colonies, including Ontario and eventually the Canadian prairies. The purpose was, of course, to facilitate the accumulation of capital by the early industrialists. The availability of cheap food translated into lower wages, regardless of the effects on the domestic economy of agriculture.

In addition to land or real estate, there has for some time been a legal recognition of ideas as property, reflected in patent and copyright law. This is now being extended to any novel or particular configuration of information that anyone wants to bother with, whether as a drug formula, a computer program, a genetic sequence or a process of genetic manipulation. This extension of the enclosure movement into the realm of ideas beyond mechanical invention should really be regarded as a form of alchemy: the transformation of ideas into *intellectual property* which can be privately owned and then legally 'protected' by means of Intellectual Property Rights.

The logic of private ownership reveals its ultimate conclusion, and perhaps its absurdity, when the information over which exclusive ownership is claimed is itself the means of production and of its own reproduction.

Information is no longer understood to be simply a passive phenomenon *about* something. It is now understood as an active phenomenon *for* something. The productive potential of information is most dramatically revealed by the fact that it is the genetic information coded in the DNA that produces (or determines) a particular protein. Thus information comes to be understood as a means of production, and the owners of capital insist that it must be privatized. This is the fundamental issue behind Plant Breeders' Rights and corporate ownership of seeds.

Genetic information, the genetic coding in the chromosome that determines the life form, is regarded in the same way that a new herbicide or a new form of packaging might be. According to the theory of intellectual property rights, the researcher/inventor who comes up with a saline-resistant wheat, or rather the corporation or university that employs him or her, should be able to patent and claim as its private property the genetic information that distinguishes, *and produces*, that wheat. By the same logic, the biologist who develops a cow that is resistant or immune to mastitis should be able to patent that distinctive genetic coding. From this reductionist perspective, there is very little difference between a computer program and a set of chromosomes. Both are simply a collection of certain bits of information in a specific relationship to each other.

It is then but a short step to the patenting – claiming the property rights to – a modified human embryo, one that has been subject to gene therapy on the basis of need established as a result of amniocentesis, or some other intrusive technology, on the embryo *in utero*. In other words, once the principle of intellectual property rights is accepted, there is no natural or inherent limit to the claims that can be made. Human characteristics can be patented and licensed for production just the way a McDonald's hamburger or a new lettuce plant could be. Do you prefer curly leaves (hair) or straight, long stems (legs) or short?

In 1991 the National Institutes of Health in the United States filed patents on several hundred human gene sequences from brain tissue, followed by 2000 more patent applications early in 1992. The Medical Research Council in Britain countered by filing for patents on another 2000 sequences and the NIH upped the ante with another 4000 filings. The U.S. Patent Office rejected the NIH's first 2700 patent applications in September, 1992, questioning whether the NIH actually knew everything about the genes and whether the fragments were novel, useful and non-obvious, the three criteria for patenting. The fact is that the NIH hadn't a clue what the gene sequences were 'good for' but they argued that their utility would sooner or later be discovered. By late 1992 a truce had been called and no more patents were being filed for sequences of the human genome as researchers and others began to take seriously the implications of what they were doing.

These events took place within an established context of life-form patenting, at least in the United States, initiated in 1980 with the granting of a patent on a microorganism that liked to eat oil spills. The organism turned out to be a flop but the precedent remained, and early in 1988 the U.S. Patent Office granted Harvard University a patent on a living mouse. Actually Harvard did not get a patent on the mouse itself, but on some specific genetic material it contained as a result of genetic engineering: a gene that made the mouse susceptible to what is breast cancer in women that so that it could be used more easily in cancer research. The real significance of this for the food system is that Harvard, or the corporation to which it licensed the production rights, Monsanto, can collect royalties on the progeny of that original mouse for 17 years! All one needs to do is apply that to the hog or poultry industry to realize the potential.

The extent to which the argument for privatization can be taken is fully articulated in a study published in the United States. Addressing the question of "What biotechnological subject matter, if any, is excluded in principle from patent protection?" the authors argue that, "The basic tenet of patent law is that subject matter is in the public domain only if it is *both* old (lacks novelty) *and* obvious (lacks inventive step)". On this basis they then claim that, *"Only if it is in the public domain* should it remain free for all to use."[76]

> The patentability requirements of novelty and inventive step are sufficient to preclude the patenting of any products which are already reasonably available to man [sic]. . . the public remains free to do anything that it could have done prior to the inventor's discovery of the so- called 'product of nature'. In other words, the *actual* 'product of nature' can never be patented and does remain free for all . . .
>
> And what of the philosophical tenet that all products of nature must remain 'free for all to enjoy'? . . . As noble as this precept may sound, it is of no practical utility for promoting progress in the useful arts. . . . 'Products of nature' which are unknown to mankind are no more useful than are inventions that have not yet been made.[77]

Having virtually equated 'man-made' with any- and everything that is discovered, the authors then advise that other countries should adopt "the U.S. concept that everything under the sun that is man-made should in principle be able to enjoy the innovation-encouraging reward of patent protection".[78]

In other words, everything in the world – Creation itself – is private property waiting to be discovered, to be owned. There is nothing in the public domain until it is discovered or invented and made public through the patenting process because the public cannot enjoy what it does not know about, what has not been discovered. The Creator God, then, will have to argue His or Her case in patent court.

AGRICULTURAL TRADE AND INTELLECTUAL PROPERTY

The December, 1988, meeting of the General Agreement on Tariffs and Trade (GATT) in Montreal was an important event because, for the first time, agricultural trade was on the GATT agenda. Officially the major issues were liberalization of agricultural trade, the elimination of non-tariff barriers, the harmonization of health, safety, and packaging regulations, and intellectual property rights. At the top of the practical agenda, however, was the purported agricultural subsidy and trade war between the United States and the European Commission (EC) acting for the European Economic Community (EEC). In spite of its own massive subsidization of agricultural commodities exported through its Export Enhancement Program, the U.S.A. insisted that all responsibility for the disastrously low global grain prices lay with the agricultural export subsidies of the EC. Five years later the U.S. still makes the same claims, but from its inception in 1985 up to January, 1992, sixteen transnational corporations had received $3.58 billion in subsidies from the U.S. Government, with Cargill at the head of the list with $800 million.[79]

During this same period, while grain prices have continued to be pushed down, there is still no new global trade agreement; but the U.S. has succeeded in bludgeoning one country after another, with the threat or exercise of trade sanctions (Super 301, as it is called), into conforming with its legal interpretation of intellectual property rights. Canada, with the extension of the patent period on drugs in 1993, is the most recent (in this case, only too willing) victim.

Of the 96 or so countries participating in the GATT, 70 are what are loosely termed 'developing'. The people of these countries have interests, by and large, very different from those of the wealthy North (or what should probably, since the 'collapse of communism' in 1989, be referred to as the North-West). However, the question of *whose* interests are actually represented in GATT is quite different from that of which governments are participating. Perhaps it is a senior executive of the Swiss transnational Nestlé who is really the voice coming from the French delegation, or perhaps Argentina is advised by the Vice President of Bunge and Born, one of the five biggest global grain traders. And it may well be a senior Vice President of Cargill who sits behind the U.S. desk, along with the man from Monsanto. Certainly the voices heard in the GATT discussions are not those of the inner city poor, landless peasants, indigenous peoples, or even the increasingly marginalized middle class.

Brazil, for example, is one of the Cairns Group of 13 grain exporting countries, along with Canada, Argentina, Chile, Colombia, Australia, Hungary, Indonesia, Malaysia, New Zealand, the Philippines, Thailand and Uruguay. It is difficult to understand what the people of these countries have in common that their governments can pretend to speak with one voice. Certainly the trade representatives of the Brazilian Government do not represent the ⅔ of the Brazilian people who are hungry and without sufficient income to buy food because the resources of the country are being devoted to the development of export agriculture, hydro-electric projects in Amazonia, and payments on their massive debt of $112.5-billion to the banks of Canada, the U.S., and elsewhere.[80]

Or take the example of Sri Lanka: 200 years ago Sri Lanka was self-sufficient in food. Along came the British Empire which imposed an international division of labour: Sri Lanka would produce tea for the global market, rather than rice and textiles for itself. (The British were protecting their own textile industry, even though they had to import the cotton for it!) After the British came the Green Revolution which brought HYVs (high yielding varieties) of rice and another form of dependency; and then the U.S. with its wheat which altered their rice-based culture. Now Sri Lanka is being told to grow things like oil palms for the global market, yet another division of labour for the benefit of foreign interests.

From the Canadian perspective, we have to ask if our GATT negotiators represent the farmer members of the three Prairie Wheat Pools or the international grain traders with offices in Winnipeg and Toronto? Do they represent the dairy farmers with supply management and the rural communities of Canada, or the elite of The World Bank? The easiest way to answer the question is to look at who benefits from low grain prices, from chemical monoculture, from the public subsidies that are passed through the farmers to the banks and the seed and chemical companies, that is, who benefits from the policies of the Government and its corporate advisors.

To give a Canadian example, from 1984 to 1987, under an 'executive exchange' program, David Gilmore, a Vice President of Cargill Ltd. (the Canadian subsidiary of Cargill, Inc.), was on loan from Cargill to Agriculture Canada to assist in drafting agricultural policy for the Conservative government. Cargill continued to pay his salary while he occupied an office on the top floor of the Carling Building in Ottawa beside the Deputy Minister of Agriculture. In 1986 another Cargill employee, Phil de Kemp, under the same Executive Exchange Program, went to work in the

Grain Marketing Bureau and later became an aide to Grains and Oilseeds Minister (and Minister responsible for the Canadian Wheat Board) Charlie Mayer.

The reports from the GATT meetings give voice to those demanding the right to pursue corporate profits or a reduced deficit through the sale and export of agricultural surpluses, not those who demand fair trade and a chance to feed their own people. We do not read in the press about the profound differences between trade in agricultural goods (trading the left-overs after feeding the family) and commodity export agriculture.

Trade implies on-going relationships with trading *partners*, and to be on-going the terms of trade have to be sustainable. Sustainability requires fairness and justice between sectors in the food system as well as sustainability in supply, i.e., production.

Export, on the other hand, is essentially opportunistic, a one-way transaction that seeks to maximize returns, whether to "service" foreign debt or, as in the case of the U.S., to pay for domestic and global militarization and the latest attack on Iraq. As Canada, the U.S., the EC and others push them, agricultural exports have little or nothing to do with reciprocity or fairness. 'Comparative advantage' is precisely *not* based on sustainability or justice. The pursuit of advantage is the pursuit of power.

The Canadian government's major concern at GATT, and articulated through the Cairns Group, is the protection of our *right* to export surplus grain, but it is precisely our dependency on agricultural production for export that is destroying rural Canada. Canada's position is rationalized on the grounds that its economy as a nation-state has always depended on the export of agricultural production, particularly grains.[81]

In spite of all the discussion and propaganda about trade, export subsidies and the North American Free Trade Agreement, however, the future of food production around the world is more apt to be shaped by the issues of Intellectual Property Rights (IPR), patenting and biotechnology. The trade/export issues will be insignificant if the germplasm of every food crop and farm animal is patented by one or another of a handful of TNCs who are also the producers of agricultural chemicals: Ciba-Geigy,

Bayer, and Sandoz (Swiss), Rhône Poulenc (French), Cyanamid and DuPont (U.S.A.), BASF (German), and ICI (British).[82]

The few people or businesses actually growing the food will be reduced to the status of franchisees, dependent for all their inputs on a few corporations and also liable for royalties to the same corporations on everything they produce. The state will perform its assigned role of patent police and collection agent. If you think this sounds like a return to feudalism, you're right.

Given the role of transnational corporations in our present food system, if the U.S. continues to win its way, then the integration of the food system, from the seed to the fruit on the table, would be virtually complete. Discussions about agricultural trade would then focus on the mechanisms of royalty payments for patented swine and corn, or on inter-corporate competition in Third World markets.

A full-colour full-page ad in several 1993 issues of *The Packer*, the weekly trade paper of the North American produce industry, depicts Adam and Eve (holding a MacIntosh apple) in the garden of Eden, complete with snake and, in the background, some very large machine-cultivated monoculture fields. The caption: "And now, the second most tempting line of fruits ever to be introduced." The fine print below reads: "After a decade of development, Sun World is introducing seven unique, patented varieties of tree fruit."

The control that can be exercised by large corporations by means of intellectual property rights seems to have no limits. Moving from a patent on a product, such as a fruit or fruit tree, or even a particular type of mouse, to a patent on a process is a qualitative leap, not simply an extension of a principle, as illustrated by the patent granted to Agracetus Inc., a subsidiary of W.R. Grace and Co., for genetically-engineered cotton products. This is not just a patent on a cotton plant with particular characteristics, which would be bad enough, but because it was first to develop transgenic cotton, Agracetus claims rights to any and all transgenic cotton, regardless of which engineering technique is used. Agracetus claims that all transgenic cotton products will have to be licensed from them before they can enter the market-place. As one industry journal put it, this "may be an indication of how major corporations can use biotech patents to get propri-etary control of huge segments of agriculture."[83]

Another broad-based patent was issued early in 1993 by the U.S. Patent Office to Plant Genetic Systems (PGS) of Belgium on plants containing *Bacillus thuringiensis* (Bt) genes as well as on any method of transferring Bt genes into any plant. According to PGS, since it was the first to demonstrate that Bt genes could be engineered into plants, any company that genetically engineers Bt into most plant crops will need to negotiate a licensing agree-ment with PGS. PGS expects the patent to cover corn, soybeans, rice, wheat, cotton, canola, tomato, cabbage and potato.[84]

This sort of extension of intellectual property rights makes it clear that the intent is not the advancement of science, nor the 'improvement' of agriculture, but control, and with control, the opportunity to accumulate wealth. Whether people need the technology, whether it will lead to better global nutrition, or even whether it is scientifically sound are not considered relevant is-sues.

If the widespread inclusion of Bt genes in plants and trees leads in short order to the development of resistance to Bt in the target pests, as many people believe it has to, this again does not seem to be a serious concern to its promoters. If resistance to Bt does result, it will simply mean that a new technological fix will have to be sought, draining even more funds away from sustain-able agricultural research.

> Monsanto, for example, has spent hundreds of millions of dol-lars on the development of recombinant Bovine Growth Hor-mone. They expected to have it on the North American market in 1989. In 1992 the company wrote off $30 million worth of its rBGH inventory that was beyond its expiry date, and the drug has still not been licensed for use in dairy cows.

Calgene, the California biotech company best known for its heroic and very expensive efforts to get patented, genetically en-gineered tomatoes on the market – its Flavr Savr ageless toma-toes – is also working on canola. Calgene thinks they can engi-neer canola so that it will produce designer oils, that is, oils with very specific characteristics for very specific uses and customers. Calgene is also a company that speaks its corporate mind more clearly than most, so it is not a bad idea to take seriously what they say, since they probably articulate what a lot of others also think but do not say:

> Our objective is to control production with our partners from the production of foundation seed to the sale of the oil to our customers. We want complete control. The seed margins don't begin to cover the cost of the investments we've made in the technology. The way you capture value added is selling oil – value-added oil at a premium to customers, period. So we and our partners will maintain complete control of the process.[85]

CHAPTER 10

FEEDING THE FAMILY: CONTRADICTIONS OF CAPITALISM

From the business press and the professional and academic economists one could easily get the idea that the sole purpose of an economy is to produce goods and services. National economies are measured by Gross Domestic Product (GDP) or Gross National Product (GNP), both of which are simply sums of all the numbers that can be accumulated as to how much commerce was done, that is, how much is bought and sold. This says nothing about unpaid work, nothing about the barter or exchange economy, and nothing about distribution.

On the contrary, the GNP or GDP will go up, and the economy 'improve', if there is a giant disaster, like the flooding of the Missouri and Mississippi Rivers or the Exxon Valdez oil spill, that requires the expenditure of large sums of money for clean-up. In the same way, the more that is spent on medicine, including drugs, heroic efforts to save lives and cosmetic surgery, the better for the economy. So not only do the economic statistics tell us nothing about distribution (justice or equity), they tell us nothing about the health of the people or the society.

In fact, the more that is spent on armed guards and armies, on police and domestic 'security', the healthier the economy appears according to the stats. The more people spend on junk food and infant formula, as opposed to growing a garden and breast-feeding, and the more they drive rather than walk or ride a bicycle, the healthier the economy appears as well.

It is enough to make one think that we suffer a rather distorted notion of what an economy is really about. The word *economy* comes from the Greek meaning *household*, and refers to the way the household is organized to care for its members. An economy, quite simply, should be about how we organize our society in order to care for every member of it. This may have very little to do with how much is bought and sold, or even with how much is produced. [86]

How did we fall into such confusion?

THE INVISIBLE HAND

We justifiably take pride in the achievements of Western Civilization, or what we like to call Democracy, and the Enlightenment, by which we mean Reason and Science. The economy that has emerged from this very particular historical context, using the tools of technology and industrialization, appears to have produced impressive abundance and wealth. Unfortunately, the benefits of this economy have not been made universally available. On the contrary, these benefits have been only very unevenly distributed within the northern and western 'democratic' nations and have not reached the vast majority of people of the world.

The net transfer of wealth from the poor and indebted countries of the Third World to the wealthy of the North is well documented. Between 1982 and 1990, the most recent year for which reliable figures are available, the net resource flow from the Third World debtor countries to the 'developed' countries of the North was a bare minimum of $418 billion; six times the amount transferred to Europe under the Marshall Plan after World War Two.[87]

The wealth produced, or accumulated, by the industrial capitalist economy is often regarded, at least by conservatives, as justification of its morality. That is, the economic system must be good to have produced so much. And they would claim that it must be scientific to have worked so well. The inequities resulting from this economy are explained away: those designated as losers have not followed the rules or played the game properly.

They have arbitrarily or irrationally intervened in the scientific and rational processes and distorted their economies. Interventions motivated by concerns for justice, equity, conservation, or ecology, are dismissed, by and large, as irrational, or unaffordable. Nevertheless, the ecological and social consequences of the industrial development policy advocated by the World Bank, transnational corporations, and their agencies are increasingly being challenged by environmental organizations and broad public movements.

If the purpose of an economy is to organize the resources of a society so that the basic needs of everyone are met (needs as defined by the people themselves, not the corporate advertising agencies of the North), then what has gone wrong that the number of hungry and malnourished is growing? Has it been the failure, or the consequence, of the theory and practice of capitalism itself?

> No famine, no flood, no earthquake, no war, has ever claimed the lives of 250,000 children in a single week. Yet malnutrition and disease claim that number of child victims *every week*.[88]

The foundations were laid for the industrial revolution and the rise of rationalism and reductionism in philosophy and science two hundred years ago. Adam Smith, the patron saint of neo-conservative economists and free market capitalists, wrote *The Wealth of Nations* in 1776. His notion of "the invisible hand", which is the magic that is supposed to guide the Market Economy to function in the best interests of everyone, was first expressed in this context:

> [Every individual generally] neither intends to promote the public interest, nor knows how much he is promoting it ... he is in this case, as in many cases, led by an invisible hand to promote an end which was no part of his intention. Nor is it always the worse for society that it was no part of it. By pursuing his own interest he frequently promotes that of society more effectually than when he really intends to promote it.[89]

But Smith had no illusions about either the social relations that would result, or the moral character of those who were the leading merchant capitalists and practitioners of his philosophy of his own day:

> Wherever there is great property, there is great inequality. For one very rich man, there must be at least five hundred poor, and the affluence of the few supposes the indigence [utter poverty] of the many.[90]
>
> Civil government, so far as it is instituted for the security of property, is in reality instituted for the defence of the rich against the poor, or of those who have some property against those who have none at all.[91]

It is a cultural and political disgrace that the 'science' of economics has come now to so dominate our public life that the primary purpose of the economy and the state has become the organizing of markets for privately tendered goods, services, and capital.

The acceptance of The Marketplace as the functional organizing principle of a society is remarkable in that it has worked so badly and the cost has been so high. The affluent lifestyle of the average North American, the achievements of science and technology, the glories of military might, and the phenomenal overproduction of food, have all been based on the deprivation of the majority of the human population and the exploitation of natural resources. As the UNICEF report *State of the World's Children 1989* put it, "policies which lead to rising malnutrition, declining health services, and falling school enrolment rates are inhuman, unnecessary, and ultimately inefficient". Four years later the 1993 edition of this annual report made the simple comment, "Basic needs will not be met, and basic investments will not be made, by any invisible hand".[92]

If we attribute to economics the status of science, and if we regard the production of surplus food as a sign of the effectiveness of science and technology, then we will probably also accept the deprivation of others as the price of progress. If our fate is indeed guided by Adam Smith's 'invisible hand', then our ethical and moral concerns can be laid to rest as sentimental intrusions.

Smith, however, did not believe that self-interest necessarily coincided with the common good. "Profit hunger conflicts with public interest" in that it always aims at a monopoly, which he defined as "infamous covetousness . . . which does not shrink from terrorization and crime". The corrective, in Smith's view, was competition, but he could hardly have been expected to foresee the consequences of his theory: the ineffectiveness of competition in controlling monopoly, the extent to which the pursuit of self-interest has not fostered the common good, the inability of the Market Economy to organize and conserve resources for sustainability, and, most fundamentally, the exclusiveness of the household served.

One of Smith's contemporaries, Jeremy Bentham, recognized the consequences of the practices which Smith advocated, and, in the words of Karl Polanyi, offered this solution to the problem in an argument reminiscent of current rhetoric about social welfare programs:

> Labour should be dealt with as that which it is, a commodity which must find its price in the market. The laws of commerce were the laws of nature and consequently the laws of God. Bentham believed that poverty was part of plenty. "On the highest stage of social prosperity," he said, "the great mass of citizens will probably possess few other resources than their daily labour, and consequently will always be near to indigence".[93]

WORKERS AND CONSUMERS

Among the many contradictions of capitalism is this: on the one hand there is the persistent drive to find or develop new markets both for the products of industry and for the capital expropriated from the economy. On the other hand, there is the equally persistent drive to maximize profit by reducing costs, namely the costs of raw materials and labour. As a result, an antagonistic contradiction arises: the market consists of customers, that is, people with money to spend, while at the same time labour is paid as little as possible. The problem then is, how to sell the goods!

The top Canadian food companies spent a minimum total of $365-million in 1992 on food advertising alone, with P&G's Grocery Product Division spent $3 million of that total.[94] In 1991, Proctor & Gamble was the top spending U.S. advertiser, ahead of even Philip Morris and General Motors, spending US$2.15 billion on advertising.[95]

The very system that devotes energy and resources to developing markets at the same time reduces large numbers of the global population to a level of poverty that excludes them from the system as customers. Henry Ford knew he had to pay his workers enough to turn them into customers for his cars, and John D. Rockefeller, whose philanthropy is largely responsible for financing the research that led to the Green Revolution, knew that capitalism needed both markets and a stable, welcoming political environment. Having accumulated a vast fortune by the turn of the century, Rockefeller created the charitable trusts whose good works he hoped would neutralize the all too evident inequities of capitalism and repel the threat of socialism as an alternative.

This same philosophy led the Rockefeller Foundation to establish a research centre (CIMMYT) in Mexico for work in 'improving' wheat and maize (corn). This centre, and a few others, became world famous as the pioneers and propagators of the Green Revolution which was based on the high-yielding varieties (high-response varieties as their critics call them) of hybrid seeds developed by these research centres. The underlying agenda was the thwarting of communism and the inclusion of Third World agriculture in the market of the North.

> [A] plausible and significant reason [for the Rockefeller Foundation establishing this work] is that American foreign policy-makers in the 1940s perceived Mexico as a strategically important country . . . that needed to be modernized without a revolution and linked harmoniously to the expanding U.S. postwar economy. The official version is that the Rockefeller Foundation was persuaded . . . to do something about world hunger.
>
> As the program at CIMMYT developed, it . . . represented 'managed' social reform through strategic technical change, the hallmark of Rockefeller philanthropy. With a more 'efficient' agricultural base would come political stability and an increase in international trade, particularly, as it turned out, for the products like fertilizers, pesticides, irrigation pumps, farm machinery and fuel required to make the new agriculture work and the new plants realise their potential yields.
>
> The Rockefeller initiative was followed by other foundations such as the Ford Foundation, which helped establish an International Rice Research Institute . . . (in the Philippines).[96]

COMPETITION

The ruling axiom of Market Economy theory is that our economic ills – including hunger and malnutrition in the Third World – can only be overcome through increased efficiency and productivity: by becoming more competitive. Yet the biggest 'investments' made in the food system in the past decade were not in new or more efficient production facilities, but in take-overs and leveraged buy-outs of food processing and distributing companies. Thus businesses may change hands for billions of dollars with absolutely no investment in productivity or efficiency being made. The purpose is not to fulfil the public ideological goals of the Market Economy, but to provide a quick profit (instant gratification) for the owners, advisors and bankers.

Adam Smith would surely have difficulty reconciling the immense resulting concentration of unproductive economic power with his theory about the need for competition if the pursuit of self-interest was to actually work for the common good:

> To widen the market and narrow the competition is always the interest of the dealers . . . The proposal of any new law or regulation of commerce which comes from this order, ought always to be listened to with great precaution, and ought never to be adopted, till after having been long and carefully examined, not only with the most scrupulous, but with the most suspicious attention. It comes from an order of men, whose interest is never exactly the same with that of the public, who have generally an interest to deceive and even to oppress the public, and who accordingly have, upon many occasions, both deceived and oppressed it.[97]

An overview of our global food system reveals such immense contradictions and irrationalities that one might well wonder how the system continues to function at all. That it does is probably testimony not to its inner logic or the science of market economics, but to the immense resources and forgiveness of the Earth, whose stability and ability to absorb punishment is great enough that until recently we have been able to ignore the global consequences of our activities.

POPULATION

The Market Economy is based on the economics of scarcity, or more precisely, the dogma of scarce resources. Nature is held responsible for inequities because she is stingy and does not provide enough to go around. The other way of stating this same approach is that there are too many people. If a society does not want to address the issue of distributive or social justice – making sure that every member of the household is fed – then a theory of scarce resources and overpopulation can serve a useful function in maintaining class inequities: there simply isn't enough to go around.

The result is that there are many people who believe that unless we continue to become more productive, we will face disaster within a few decades as the growth of global population outstrips the growth in the food supply. This argument has been put forward by the same class of people since the days of The Rev. Thomas Malthus 200 years ago. Their argument has been consistent: poor people tend to multiply at a higher rate than rich people, and left unchecked *they* will multiply beyond the ability of the earth to provide for them. Thus the poor are themselves believed to be the cause of their own poverty. Malthus recognized that those who could afford to have many children refused to do so, but he never drew any conclusions from this observation. Two hundred years later it is still those who hold the wealth and power, and those who identify with them, no matter how poor they are, who seem to be the ones most worried about the deprived of the world multiplying. One can hardly help but conclude that their arguments and advice, and even policies, are more protectionist than charitable.

Human reproduction rates are, in fact, closely correlated with economic well-being: the harder the circumstances, the more children a family will have in order to have more breadwinners and to ensure that there will be enough that survive to care for the elderly. The easier the circumstances, the smaller the families, and until a woman can be reasonably sure that all her children will survive, it does not make economic sense to her to limit her family. As a study done for the Brundtland Commission expressed it, "The problem is not one of global food production being outstripped by population . . . . The problem has three aspects: where the food is being produced, by whom, and who can command it."[98]

The constantly shifting definition of *family*, in practice if not in public ideology or theory, should be a healthy reminder of the danger of a single arbitrary definition of family and of social responsibility. A healthy economy, with a healthy community, will care for everyone within its physical domain with a reasonable degree of equity. (The Deuteronomic Code called, as did Jesus in turn, for including the widow, the orphan, the alien and the sojourner.) One could describe this as enlightened self-interest, for who knows when *we* might find ourselves on the outside – but self-interest of a very different sort than that encouraged by capitalism and the Market Economy.

CHAPTER 11

FROM COW TO COMPONENT

THE EFFICIENT COW

Efficient, Productive, and *Competitive* are the three magic words of the Modern Market Economy. They are being used to facilitate the reduction of agriculture to a lifeless industrial process under the control of a limited number of transnational corporations. Dairying is a good example.

The Canadian Holstein is *productive.* In Canada the dairy industry is also highly organized and very *efficient*, largely due to the leading role played by provincial milk marketing boards and commissions (which are *not* profit-oriented businesses) and by supply management. (Supply management is the practice of tailoring supply to demand by having an agency, such as a milk marketing board, license farmers to produce milk and controlling supply through quotas.)

Unfortunately, despite such initiatives to achieve equity in the marketplace, the structures of the dairy industry appear to be dominated by the technological determinism of the industrial society, in both Canada and the U.S. Little resistance and virtually no alternatives have been offered to the ideology of production and efficiency at any and all costs. Nowhere is this clearer than in the acceptance by the dairy organizations (*not* the farmers) of the corporate agenda as expressed in the ' technology' of recombinant Bovine Growth Hormone. (We will come back to this shortly.)

As for *competitive*, the Holstein cow is probably a little more so than a Jersey or a Hereford cow, although Holstein psychology has not yet given firm indications of how inherently competitive they are. In terms of productivity, the tremendous increases that have been achieved with Holstein cows as producers of skim milk are impressive, but these gains are also probably the greatest threat to the Holstein's true competitiveness. To become 'competitive' in the industrial-economic sense, the Holstein has been forced to become so dependent on the farmer, his machinery, and his purchased protein concentrates, if not feed, that she would quickly turn into a wreck if left to fend for herself in the way most beef or dual-purpose brood cows rightly are.

The dairy industry is among the most high-tech sectors of the food system: technological intervention affects the breeding of the cow, her feeding, her milking, and finally the processing of her milk.

For the sake of genetic improvement and gains in productivity, not even breeding is simply breeding anymore. It is a contrived process of selection and manipulation that could conceivably see a cow give birth to a calf that was put together in a lab out of patented genetic material from a dead bull and a dead cow. As it is now, dairy cows are seldom bred directly by a bull, who is, instead, usually kept at a special facility where his semen can be collected by technological means, frozen, and then transported and inserted into a particular cow for a fee. Due to this very effective distancing, the cow may never see a bull in her entire life. She will live in a unisexual world alongside other black and white production machines.

A step beyond AI (artificial insemination) is embryo transplantation, where embryos are flushed from the desired dam, fertilized by the sire of choice, and then reinserted in the same or another cow. A further refinement of this process is the flushing of multiple embryos and their insertion in a number of cows after fertilization. An even further refinement can be taken by splitting an embryo, fertilizing the embryo fractions, growing them a bit and then inserting them into the cows chosen to produce, not their own offspring, but the identical products of human construction. The outcome could be a whole milking herd of genetically identical cows. The whole herd might then be replaced either when the price for slaughter cows was right or when there was a price advantage to a new model cow. It's the cow as automobile, from assembly line to scrap yard.

This new model might be one capable of producing, not milk specifically for human consumption, but milk containing a valuable drug as a result of yet more genetic manipulation along the way so that the cow becomes a pharmaceutical factory – what might be called 'pharming.' The drug would be reclaimed from the milk, leaving the milk to be disposed of in any number of ways, including human consumption. Why not? – we're already drinking milk that is homogenized, pasteurized, skimmed, vitamin enriched and possibly soon even irradiated!

The feed for this production machine may itself have been genetically engineered, not necessarily to be more nutritious, but to be more resistant to leaf miner or a nematode, or to a particular herbicide or insecticide. This engineered feed can be augmented – or perhaps this would be better stated as, the cow's metabolic processes can be enhanced – by various manufactured substances such as hormones and antibiotics, again in the name of productivity and efficiency. If the cow manages to be long-lived in spite of all this, she will be fortunate indeed, because the average number of lactations for a Holstein in North America is now about 2½, meaning that she is four years old when sold for hamburger. Given that old-fashioned cows could easily milk for 8 to 12 years, modern production practices do not appear to be very efficient, although it is claimed that the price for four-year-old Holsteins as cow-beef does make this financially attractive when balanced against the cost of replacement heifers and the returns on milk. Being financially attractive in a certain situation does not, however, necessarily make the practice either efficient or sustainable.

If our Holstein cow is thus being continuously 'improved', the question that must be asked is, what is the net gain to society, if any, resulting from this supposed gain in efficiency?

As the word is used today, efficiency refers to the ratio between inputs and outputs. To make any sense, of course, the inputs and outputs have to be carefully described as to character, amounts, and cost. In a capitalist culture, efficiency is usually evaluated in terms of short-term *numerical* efficiency, that is, the costs of inputs relative to the price of the output. This numerical efficiency deals only with the current use and configuration of the parts, not with the functioning of the whole, either on its own or in relation to others, or over the long term.

Even within the context of short-term numerical efficiency, being more efficient can, in part, be attributed to the practice of shifting certain costs from the accounting of the seller to that of the buyer, for example, by eliminating home delivery. The milk still has to get from the store or dairy to the home, and there is a cost to someone in that effort. The externalizing of certain costs is not the same thing as actually becoming more efficient, that is, getting the milk from the cow to the consumer with the least gross expenditure of energy, according to the thermodynamic law of efficiency. (see Chapter 14.)

Once the cost of getting the milk to the consumer directly has been replaced by the lower cost of delivering the milk to the retail store (very few delivery destinations), the cost to consumers goes up because they still have to take the time to get the milk (among other things) from the store. There is in this, as well, the assumption that there is a person available to take the time to pick up the milk: in the current reality this becomes yet another stress on the typical single, often female, head of the household and/or wage-earner. Socially, as well as economically, this may actually be seriously inefficient.

> In Stratford, Ontario, Avon Dairy now delivers milk to your door by means of a wagon drawn by two horses. There are two delivery persons dressed in the traditional uniform and bow tie, a bucket and scoop for picking up after the horses, and the wagon is insulated. It is quite a surprise – and delight – to come upon this without warning! In Vancouver, Avalon Dairy never gave up on glass bottles, and now most of the dairies in the Vancouver area offer milk in returnable glass bottles.

The same false efficiency operates at the other end of the dairy system. As the number of dairy farms and dairy processors has decreased, the distances the milk has had to be hauled have increased. This process of reducing the number of farms and the number of dairies in the name of efficiency is referred to, again, as 'rationalization'. As a result, milk hauling may cost the dairies and the farmers less, but that will be in part because the cost of the highways over which the milk is hauled, including snowplowing, is paid for by the public.

The corporation, the enterprise, or the individual that is most successful in externalizing their costs is likely to be the winner in the Market Economy. One prize will probably be public subsidies in one form or another, in spite of their vociferous pieties for the Free Market.

> For example, look at Cargill Inc. of Minneapolis, the world's largest private corporation with 800 subsidiaries in 55 countries. Cargill has never let its very public voice for 'free enterprise' stand in the way of accepting public subsidies, whether in the form of a $4.5-million grant from the Government of Alberta towards the costs of its beef packing plant at High River, or $800 million in Export Enhancement Program subsidies from the U.S. Government from 1985 through 1991. There is nothing special about Cargill, however; this is common practice, though Cargill may have its hand deeper into the public pocket than most.

Within this logic, 'competitive' describes the character of social relations between individuals seeking what is best for themselves. Those that are successful, the winners, are by definition 'efficient'. If, as a result, some people get rich and others starve, that is regarded as an unfortunate consequence of an efficient market economy, not a moral issue.

> The social ideology of bourgeois society is that the individual is ontologically prior to the social. Individuals are seen as freely moving social atoms, each with his or her own intrinsic properties, creating social interactions as they collide in space. Society as a phenomenon is the outcome of the individual activities of individual human beings.[99]

The premise of a Market Economy – that the individual pursuit of personal gain will result in the greatest good for the greatest number – is a matter of faith, and it only makes sense in the context of the reductionist logic that the whole is nothing more than the sum of its parts. As soon as we raise our sights, however, we can see that this individualism is anything but efficient, and is, in fact, leading to global ecological disaster.

MARKETING TECHNOLOGICAL WONDERS

Trade shows can be fun. They are intended to sell new technology, new equipment, and new services, and to provide a networking opportunity. They also provide a wonderful display of the character of an industry and where it is going. The 1991 Food and Dairy Expo in Chicago focused on low fat, no fat, and natural. The 1987 show focused on packaging and an apparent diversity of products, such as the diversity of ice cream novelties that satisfied my need for lunch for two days.

Since fancy ice cream is a big money-spinner, the 1991 show, like the 1987 one, featured flavours and fruits, ice milks and non-dairy ices, yogurts and rich ice creams, along with the very expensive gleaming technology required to mix, sterilize, pack and freeze the fluids and forms.

Among the manufacturers of dairy processing, packaging, and handling equipment, ingredient suppliers (nuts, frozen fruits, flavours, extenders, emulsifiers, etc.) and related corporate interests present at the 1987 show was Cargill. Cargill was present under two flags: as a manufacturer of a Maltose corn-based sweetener and as recent purchaser of a Dutch chocolate company. The Dutchman at a chocolate display explained that he understood that Cargill bought his company because Cargill is after 25% of every food commodity on the world market.

At the 1991 show Cargill presented its orange juice face as a global leader in the production, concentration and bulk delivery of frozen orange juice.

Cargill is not the only peddler of sweeteners. The most aggressively marketed artificial sweetener is NutraSweet. NutraSweet is the trade name for a patented form of aspartame made by G.D. Searle, a subsidiary of Monsanto Corporation, one of the chemical giants that has moved heavily into biotechnology and other 'value-added' lines, including its infamous synthetic form of Bovine Growth Hormone.

With the looming expiration of its patent on aspartame, Monsanto has continued to wage an advertising war on any and all competitors. Of course, one should remember that it is the consumer who ultimately foots the bill for all such advertising.

In its promotional material NutraSweet is described as "the only sweetener made from protein components . . . . It is made of two protein components (amino acids) . . . found naturally in a variety of foods". Does that make it a natural product? The manufacturers do not claim that it is, but it raises the interesting question about what is natural at a time when new processes are being discovered almost daily to engineer new products out of naturally occurring substances.

Another wonder is Solka-Floc, described in company promotion as, "a family of finely divided fibrous products manufactured from purified cellulose . . . the ideal ingredient for the food industry because it has no flavour or odour, is essentially non-caloric, and contains at least 99% dietary fibre". The sales rep did not hesitate to explain that the product probably came from Canadian maple, beech, or birch. At home we call it wood pulp. Its advantage over bran is that it does not tie up (or 'bind') essential minerals as it passes though the digestive tract. How natural can you get!

Also at the 1987 show was BiPRO, described in a company brochure as, "the first of a new generation of dairy ingredients that combine enhanced functionality, full solubility, and neutral flavour. BiPRO is a wholly natural ingredient produced from pasteurized whey through selective ion exchange. The unique ion-exchange process selects out the main functional proteins . . . for concentration and spray-drying . . . . Good taste, good nutrition, increased profits; they're all yours with BiPRO enriched beverage products."

Olestra is a example of both the costs and what are seen to be the ultimate profits of getting synthetic or substitute food products onto the market. Olestra is intended as a non-fat fat substitute in food manufacturing. It has been under development for 25 years by Proctor & Gamble at a cost, they say, of $200 million, and it has still not been approved for use commercially.[100]

TECHNOLOGICAL PROCESSES

Some of the most intriguing new technology is for filtration, with new developments of old technology now able to purify even the most noxious waste, though not necessarily cheaply. These filtration processes utilize polymer and ceramic filters that can filter out, or allow to pass through the filter in a continuous process, molecules of specified weights, or sizes. Thus there is low-pressure ultrafiltration, high pressure reverse osmosis, and gas permeation under vacuum. Not only is this technology capable of discharging post-manufacturing-process water that is probably cleaner than the city water that went into the system, it can also separate food into even more discriminate components than other methods developed thus far.

Some of the applications of ultrafiltration, which is a relatively low-energy technology, are in milk concentration (water removal) for cheese-making, concentration of whey, clarification and concentration of fruit juices, water purification, and concentration of maple sap. Gay Lea, a farmer's dairy cooperative in Ontario, has an ultrafiltration system in one of its plants that extracts valuable protein components from the whey produced by its cheese-making, turning what has been a polluting, unusable waste into usable components and clean water.

The potential implications of this technology are a challenge to the imagination. Like virtually all new food processing technology, it is designed as a continuous-flow process. A good example of continuous-flow is CIP (Clean In Place): dairy equipment, from pipeline milkers to pasteurizing and packaging machinery, are cleaned without dis-assembly by washing cleaning agents through the continuous system.

The reduction of a whole product, such as milk, into its components (fats, non-fat solids, water, etc.) by a relatively inexpensive process is very appealing, and it is consistent with the trend in the food system to gain as much flexibility as possible for those in control. Breaking the raw materials down into essential components for subsequent recombination into as many different products as possible, in turn facilitates centralization of processing, distribution, and corporate control. Food production begins

to take on the characteristics of 'world-class' electronics production: a handful of corporations source their components around
the world and ship them by the container-load to the market region for final assembly into several different models. 'Natural'
components can thus be used instead of synthetic ones to assem-
ble 'natural' industrial foods.

> We should take a new look at milk, and use technology in our
> industry the way it is frequently used in other industries, that
> is, instead of saying milk is the end, say milk is the beginning.
> What is milk?   Milk is simply the agglomeration of con-
> stituents. Let's break it down and recombine it in as many
> ways as we can.[101]

The potential reduction of whole milk into fractions, or components, parallels the reduction of corn into components engineered for certain purposes, such as the maltose described above.
Add other developments in food science, like the discovery of new
enzymes and new uses for them, and it appears likely that the
marketing engineers may soon be *the only ones* deciding the
forms of food that we will eat.

> Industrial research and development is revealing the molecular
> composition of food in all its aspects, from its behaviour in in-
> dustrial processing to the biochemical determinants of flavour
> . . . Due to fractionation and industrial reconstitution, [the
> food] system has become much more complex with more inter-
> mediate processing steps separating field and table. Thus the
> final food product may be at several removes from its original
> rural form.[102]
>
> These advanced techniques threaten to *trivialize* agricul-
> ture, transforming it into one among several competing sources
> of organic matter for biomass conversion and fractionation.[103]

Accompanying these developments in production technology are new food preservation and packaging techniques. Food
packaging and preservation has been around as long as food itself:
storing in brine, canning, cold cellars, even simply leaving it in
the ground (or in the ice in the north) for storage. But the precise
tailoring of food design, processing, and packaging is now reach-
ing levels of sophistication that would have been unimaginable
even one generation ago.

A major breakthrough came in the early 1950s from the

Swedish company Tetra Pak (see Chapter 3) with the idea of aseptic (sterile) carton packaging, but this technology only really hit its stride in the 1980s. Aseptic packaging is a process whereby a food, in liquid form (mostly juices and dairy products), is put into a sterile package in a chamber of sterile (filtered) air. Hydrogen peroxide is the sterilizing agent because it breaks down as water and is absorbed as soon as it has done its job.

Combined with Ultra High Temperature pasteurization ('UHT' in Canada, 'Ultra Pasteurization' in the U.S.) of the milk or juice, which virtually sterilizes the product, aseptic packaging provides extremely long shelf life. (Refrigerated shelf life can be increased from 16-18 days to 30-45 days.) While the elimination of preservatives is a plus, the minus is the package itself, a laminate containing inseparable, and hence unrecyclable, metal, plastic, and paper film. Tetra Pak has spent a lot of money in recent years trying to deal with this problem, and now offers park benches, among other things, made from recycled 'drinking boxes'. "True to Nature – keeping food in good shape" reads a Tetra Pak ad.

In 1992, the Rausing family, owners of Tetra Pak, bought out the venerable Swedish dairy equipment manufacturer Alfa Laval at a cost of about $3 billion. Alfa Laval is to dairy equipment what Sears-Roebuck used to be to the outhouse. From vacuum lines to bulk tanks, from cream separators to robotic milkers, Alfa Laval's gleaming stainless steel equipment has been around as long as there has been a 'dairy industry'.

The new company, Tetra Laval, was described by its president as "the world's strongest industrial group aimed at the food industry". Its c.e.o., Hans Rausing, said his main business goal is the provision of a complete range of food processing and packaging systems from farmer to consumer, something which "no other company in the world has yet been capable of doing".

Such a company can exercise immense control over the distance from cow to consumer, and as a privately-owned company there is little we can do to influence its policy choices that will effect us. We can and have, however, contributed to the welfare of its owners, who can now claim a family wealth of $8 billion dollars.[104]

Maybe a company like Tetra Laval can now be said to deliver milk from teat to table, but we used to do the same thing on the farm by means of a milk bucket carried between barn and house. Unpasteurized and unhomogenized, but clean and refrigerated, the milk from our family cow was central to a healthy diet and a healthy family.

What all this 'continuous flow' does for distancing, centralization, and concentration in the food industry should be obvious, but what effect this sterilization of food has on nutrition is less obvious. So far, sterility seems to be regarded as an unmitigated good in the food processing industry. Cleanliness must be next to godliness and a long shelf life. "The future may even see hospital operating-room-type conditions in the handling of milk from farmer to consumer. I call this managing the environment," says a U.S. dairy industry executive.

On the other hand, as our analytical techniques become increasingly refined, we may discover that there is indeed some material basis for the contention that even traditional pasteurization destroys some of the more subtle nutritional qualities of milk. We might also come to learn that homogenization is not as innocent a process as claimed, since it does alter the size and character, and hence digestibility, of the fat globules in milk. Instead of being outlawed, the consumption of unpasteurized, unhomogenized milk from within the local bioregion (so the system is not being challenged by foreign 'bugs') may one day be prescribed by health professionals and even doctors.[105]

What we may discover, long after considerable cumulative damage has been done, is that the more we sterilize and kill what we eat – what goes into our bodily material composition – the weaker and more dependent we become as a living organism, very much like highly bred dairy cows, hybrid corn or HRV rice. We really know very little about the subtle and complex relations both among the various functions of our bodies and between these functions and our environment. Every step we take to 'clean up our act' may, in fact, be deleterious in ways we cannot yet describe but should be able to imagine.

Healthy, living food tastes better, lasts longer, and is more nutritious than food that has been poisoned, embalmed and shipped around the world. An organic gardener who sells very fancy salads to elite restaurants told me that she no longer uses any hybrid seeds because she found that the open-pollinated varieties provide better-tasting greens with a longer shelf-life. I know, as well, that untreated, organically grown potatoes will keep a lot longer than conventional chemical/industrial potatoes. Potatoes treated with sprout inhibitor (maleic hydrazide or chlorpropham) may produce few sprouts, stay firmer and look better – up to a point – but they don't taste as good and are probably not as nutritious as sprouted and even wizened organic potatoes.

BIOTECHNOLOGY

Biotechnology, as created by capitalist business culture, is an interventionist program to gain greater control over the productive process. It deals primarily in the genetic information controlling both process and product which, as we have seen, becomes itself a means of production. That is, genetic engineering is an extension of the drive of rationalist and capitalist culture to gain ever greater control over the means of production in the pursuit of profit.

Going back to the Holstein model discussed earlier, it is clear that genetic information is crucial in every step of the process. Certain genetic information is selected, by a variety of processes, in order to produce a cow with specific characteristics. The alfalfa or corn she feeds on has also been genetically selected or engineered in order to produce a crop with specific characteristics. The resulting corn or alfalfa then itself becomes the means of producing the milk in the cow.

Once the cow has been milked, the milk itself becomes the object of other processes of biotechnology, such as breaking the milk down into its constituent components so that it can be engineered into some new food. This process of breaking down and recombination is itself a matter of manipulating genetic material (information), which continues to be a factor of production.

The farmer may think that he or she is in charge of the farm and this is certainly encouraged by the Ag Reps, bankers, economists, and others. But if we stop to reconsider our Holstein cow, we can see that the farmer is increasingly bound to play a pre-defined role within the productive process genetically engineered into the cow, the feed, and the milk itself. As Robert Doyle put it, "farmers are becoming tenders of genes they do not control".[106]

The farmer turns out to be only a *rentier*: the real means of production are the genes, chromosomes, and germplasm which are rented out to the farmer in the form of various genetic packages, like seed, cow, and herbicide. Were efficiency, and not control, the real interest of the owners of the means of production, then the genetic design and engineering department would pursue different goals. Doyle describes the emerging situation as "a coupling of genetic power with corporate power".

Until very recently, virtually all agricultural research in both Canada and the United States was carried out in public institutions – universities or government research agencies – with public money. During the past decade, however, there has been mounting pressure from corporate interests and their representatives in government to privatize all of the commercially attractive results. They want the public to continue to pay for the basic research (for which there is no direct financial return) while the private sector appropriates and commercializes whatever fruits the research bears.

One of the best means of capitalizing on public research is to obtain patents and licenses on the commercial or potentially commercial results. And as we discussed in Chapter 9, when what is being patented is genetic information which is now available as a means of production, the logic of the private ownership of the means of production is complete.

Why is there no great public debate about this expropriation of public resources through the assertion of the doctrine of Intellectual Property Rights?

> The first line of defense of the status quo is always ideology; if people believe that the existing social order, whatever its inequalities, is inevitable and right, they will not question it. In this way, ideologies become a material force.[107]

Modern science and capitalism both depend on the passivity

of the majority of the population: profits are reduced to the extent that there is resistance to exploitation. Resistance may take the simple form of a strike (where not instigated by the company for its own purposes) or it may take the form of a land occupation or the sabotage of equipment that is to displace labour. The corporate/state response may be simple police/army intervention, or, as in many countries, more harsh measures by private assassins or para-military death squads. Starvation is not regarded as sufficient reason for peasants to seize land or organize for collective bargaining if it interferes with the pursuit of profits.

However, it is much cleaner and more efficient if we all accept Science and Technology (the two words always appear together like Siamese twins) as the evolving self-determining phenomena to which we must adapt and over which we have, and can have, no control. Hence the propagation of technological determinism as a tool of the controlling interests. (In the next chapter we will examine the origins of this.)

There is another rationale for the increasing role of genetic engineering in agriculture and food production: biotechnology is touted as a way to reduce agricultural input costs and reduce the role of agricultural chemicals. This is attractive at a time when increasing food production *per se* is no longer the primary concern of most agricultural economists or food policy bureaucrats. The new official position is: produce the same amount of food more efficiently. (If efficiency equals output over input, then efficiency can be increased by holding output steady while decreasing input costs.) This doctrinal revision allows the agricultural economists to maintain their authoritative positions but does not change the reality of the primary producer.

Biotechnology is touted as the new way for the primary producer to avoid the traditional trap of trying to produce more in the vain hope of getting ahead, an effort which, in a saturated market, simply leads to a lower price. Producing the same amount, or less, but at lower costs, should increase net returns. This is the promise of biotechnology, but it is just what has been promised to farmers for generations by those who control the terms of trade. Any increases in genuine efficiency by the primary producer are quickly taxed away by those who have effective control over the inputs and the market. In addition, any momentary advantage gained by one producer through the adoption of new technology is soon eliminated as other producers adopt the same technology. This turns into an endless quest for advantage through new technology: the 'technology treadmill.' The real beneficiaries continue to be the manufacturers and salesmen of the technology and the information.

If greater efficiency – producing at lower real costs – is really the goal, then one would seek to actually eliminate a cost, like the herbicide, rather than making the production process dependent on the increasing costs of sophisticated technology. This is what Monsanto is doing with the development of plant varieties that are resistant to its herbicide Roundup in order to expand the market for the herbicide.

Greater efficiency, clearly, is not the guiding principle it is claimed to be. Maximization of profit (and with it control) through maximization of interventions, and hence distance between raw food and consumer, is the purpose of the industrial capitalist food system. But how did we come to find this acceptable?

CHAPTER 12

SCIENCE TAKES CONTROL

SIMPLIFICATION

The proponents of biotech-chemical-industrial agriculture frequently deride their critics by pointing out that we cannot go back to the good old days. The inference is that we have become much too sophisticated, and life much too complex, to *go back*. The fact is, however, that simplification and oversimplification are among the major characteristics of our present high-tech computerized and capitalized food system. Farming was much more complex and diverse just 40 years ago than mainstream agriculture is today; and traditional polyculture, which once supported whole populations where now we find starvation, was infinitely more complex than the simplistic solutions of plantation agriculture, the Green Revolution, and biotechnology.

> The practice of growing many crops, and even many varieties of the same crop, within the same field ensures against famine. The chances of several different crops and varieties all being destroyed simultaneously by the same pest or change in climate is remote. This is the agriculture of security rather than commerce.[108]

INPUTS UP, DIVERSITY DOWN

Superficially, our technological culture appears increasingly complex. One manifestation of this is the growing number of synthesized chemicals used in agricultural production: in mid-1993 there were 3000 pesticides on the market in Canada. 'Pesticides' includes herbicides, fungicides, insecticides, plant growth regulators, and biologicals. These 3000 products are made from approximately 335 active ingredients. In addition there are 2690 antimicrobials in use and 3898 'traditionals'. If domestic (household) and other products are included, the figures rise to 6578 total products and 479 different active ingredients.[109] Actually the term 'active ingredient' is being replaced, along with the misleading term 'inert', by the common term 'formulant' to reflect the current view that there is actually no such thing as a biologically 'inert' substance. 'Inert' was used until recently to describe anything that was "not designed to control the pest the product was designed to control".[110]

We have already described a very similar apparent complexity or diversity at the other end of the food system in the grocery store. This apparent diversity is also reflected in the complexity of farm machinery or of various diets. The impression is certainly not one of simplification, yet the major cultural aspect of modern industrial agriculture is monoculture, the growing of a single variety of a single species continuously on a vast scale accompanied by the elimination of every competitor, plant or animal or human. It is what Professor Jack Harlan referred to as "a pure line mentality, convinced that variation was bad, uniformity was good, and all off-types in the field somehow immoral".[111] Harlan was referring to the development of pure lines of crops that could then be crossed to produce hybrids. Compare this to a polyculture where every bit of solar energy, water, earth and space are utilized in an intricate web of production and survival.

The aversion to diversity is reflected in the narrowing of the genetic base that has come with the 'modernisation' of agriculture and, more recently, the Green Revolution. For example, while it is estimated that throughout human history over 3000 plant species have been used for food, most of the world's food now comes from 20 species[112] (as we have noted – see Chapter 5). However, the huge variation *within* species is essential to food security, as well, and it is this variation that is lost in the pursuit of 'improved' or hybrid varieties. It is estimated that during the past 50 years Indian farmers may have grown over thirty thousand varieties of rice, but soon it is probable that only ten varieties will cover as much as 75% of the rice-growing acreage in India,[113] while in the U.S. only 3% of varieties of 75 vegetables have survived this century. In the Andes, 60 or more varieties of potatoes are still grown.

When it comes to farm animals, the same situation holds as with crops. There may be 3350 known breeds of agricultural animals in the world, including 800 breeds of cattle and 400 breeds of pigs, but in North America you will be hard pressed to find anything other than Holstein (or Holstein-Friesen) dairy cows, half a dozen beef breeds, and a like number of hogs. Certainly to the urban North American, Holstein black and white *is* cow.

Poultry, almost all hybridized, is controlled by only 22 major breeding companies in the world, and approximately one egg in three around the world is derived from Shaver breeding stock (owned by Institut de Sélection Animale of the French Mérieux Group).[114]

The simplifications that we are most apt to overlook, because they are so obvious, are the elimination of the mixed, or diversified, farm and its replacement by a commercial monoculture production unit managed by a 'farm businessman' or a professionally trained 'agriculturalist', accompanied by a reduction in the number of farmers and the consolidation of farms.

In earlier chapters we have observed these manifestations of the logic of simplification, but observing the consequences alone can induce the kind of passivity or fatalism that the advocates of such simplification desire. Therefore it is necessary to probe more deeply, to explore the inner character of this logic, its history, and the sources of its power. Why is Science and Technology imbued with almost mystical authority in our culture today? Why is it considered appropriate to be cynical about politics, opportunistic about career paths, and ideologically rigid about economics? Why is the destructive course of industrial agriculture pursued as the only possible choice lying between us and starvation while millions go hungry? Or, as Langdon Winner puts it,

> Why has a culture so firmly based upon countless sophisticated
> instruments, techniques, and systems remained so steadfast in

its reluctance to examine its own foundations? Much of the answer can be found in the astonishing hold the idea of 'progress' has exercised on social thought during the industrial age. In the 20th century it is usually taken for granted that the only reliable sources for improving the human condition stem from new machines, techniques, and chemicals.[115]

REDUCTIONISM

In the philosophy of science, the idea that the whole is nothing but the sum of its parts, and that the project of science is to understand and explain the universe in terms of its essential parts, is called Reductionism. It claims that matter can be reduced to a catalogue of its components. This philosophy of science can also be described as linear. A line is simply a series of points, or the sum of a number of points or dots, and is described in terms of its length, which is the total of the units of measurement: so-many millimetres or kilometres. Science adds up the bits to find out how long the line is and notes the direction it is taking; the relationships between the bits are then described in terms of distance and direction. Reductionist science consists of determining the size and number and spatial configuration of the constituent parts of the universe and its contents.

The notion of Progress, which we often understand as growth, is a product of this linear logic. If we apply the logic of reductionist science to history, culture, and life, it then seems natural for us to make the assumption that the line – of history, culture, life – on which we are living will not end with us, but be carried forward by us. Like Progress, 'forward' is a word that creeps in because of our self-centredness or anthropomorphism. We naturally describe the direction that we are going in, the continuation of *our* line, as forward, or progress, since we cannot conceive, or admit, that we might actually be going backwards. 'Backward', after all, is a negative value, a moral pejorative.

Notice how the term 'improved' is used by scientists to describe many things of dubious value, including new herbicide-tolerant or hybrid seeds, as if 'improved' were an objective, scientific term. Across Canada there are 'crop improvement' associations, but what is being pushed is not improvement but the adoption of certain industrial techniques and methodologies. Since Progress is the moralization of linearity, it is immoral – or even unpatriotic – not to go forward, or to even suggest going sideways or even backwards. Any suggestion of not seizing on the latest technology is greeted with cries of "Luddite!"

> The Luddites were "An important anti-technology movement in nineteenth-century England," says Jerry Mander in his recent book, *In The Absence of the Sacred*. "Huge numbers of workers in cottage industries went on a rampage against the introduction of mass-production equipment, particularly within the textile trades." Mander goes on to cite comments made by Langdon Winner on the subject: "I am delighted to be called a Luddite. The position of the Luddites was in every way wise and perceptive. They opposed the imposition of a new economic order, which they predicted would destroy their livelihood and traditions, and lead the world in a destructive direction. They were correct. Their resistance should be an inspiration."[116]

The continuous flow phenomenon discussed in Chapter 8 is a literal expression of linearity. So is distancing, which is simply lengthening the line, both in time and space. Likewise, concentration of control requires an up-and-down hierarchical, linear structure. Monoculture, too, is linear in its essential logic. My own pleasure in seeing perfectly straight rows of a crop in a field barren of any confusion (weeds) is an expression of this same linearity.

While it may be obvious that linearity is essentially reductionist, it is less obvious that it is also determinist. If science, indeed Creation, is linear, then our only choice is to find our place in the line, or line-up. If the whole is the sum of its parts, and we are only a part, then our existence is validated only when we accept our given role in society, the whole. This proper role is itself, according to reductionist logic, determined by the sum of our determinative parts, our genes. Since we inherit these, according to this view of science, in a linear manner from our forebears, we have no choice. Therefore if we are obedient to the natural laws (some may prefer to say, for the sake of their self-respect, if we observe the natural laws) we will take our place without objection in the line-up of life. Those ahead of us are clearly superior, and those behind clearly inferior. We will be rewarded accordingly as winners or losers.

Another dimension is added to this logic by tilting the line, that is making it go up – and consequently, down. Now both ahead and above are superior positions, while behind or below are inferior, by definition.

The trickle-down theory of development follows logically. The theory is based on a hierarchical model of society. Development begins at the top with those most likely to adopt new ways (adapt to an alien culture) or new technology, and to take advantage of new opportunities, or of their neighbours. Aid goes to those who will make best use of it: the entrepreneurs who are already at the top, whether by reason of skill, inheritance, or opportunism. Development will then flow down the social structure, according to the theory. Imagine a long line of people waiting in line at the village well. The most efficient or successful is at the head of the line with the bucket. He drinks what he wants and passes the bucket back to the next in line, and so on. This is trickle-down. Or one could take the case of a well put on the rich man's land by an international aid agency, or the World Bank, because he is the one most likely to take full advantage of the water. Once his crops have been irrigated, what water is left will flow down to the next, and so on. Incredibly, this is actually the situation in many places where development aid has been given as if there were no class or social structure.

Socio-biology is a fairly recent extension of this reductionist logic. It projects personal determinism onto the whole of society: the biology of the organism is the biology of the society. Not only is our own self determined by our genes, which are inherited, so also is society determined by the genetic composition of the persons that constitute it. This effectively eliminates the need, or possibility, of democracy, since biologically there is no real possibility – or responsibility – for choice. Socio-biology thus provides a philosophical foundation, supposedly based in science, for authoritarian rule, if not fascism.

SCIENCE SUPPLANTS THEOLOGY

In the course of the history of applied science, religion has yielded authority to science, and science has been largely content to accept an authoritarian role in an otherwise secular society. Many would claim that science now serves the social purposes of medieval religion in the creation of a new feudalism.

René Descartes (1596-1650) is generally credited with inaugurating this philosophical orientation. He advocated inductive reasoning: reasoning that proceeds from the particular to the general, from the parts to the whole. Isaac Newton (1642-1727 – Newtonian physics) and others carried this line of reasoning further and developed reductionist science as the dissection of Creation, the reduction of life to its identifiable bits and pieces. The character of the whole is then induced from a description of its parts and the laws governing their relationships. God as the great watchmaker emerged; the universe could be understood by taking the clock apart and identifying its component parts. God was assigned the role of prime mover, the force that made the rules, put it all together, wound it up, and retired.

Of course the acceptance of this situation did not go quite so smoothly. Civil and religious authorities alike felt threatened by the new definitions of reality and appealed to their Divine Right: God the clockmaker had put them in their positions of authority in order to ensure the continued functioning of the great clock and to maintain social order. The maintenance of order seems always to be regarded as a divinely granted responsibility, at least by those benefitting from the order maintained!

But the sword of reductionist science was two-edged. Instead of secularism being contained by the ecclesiastical authorities, the new rationalism found it logical to marginalize God on the one hand, while on the other hand revolutionaries claimed authority for their actions as being the expression of the divine intent. While such conflicts have often led to bloody battles and exterminations, the 19th century was more polite. A compromise was worked out to the apparent benefit of both science and religion.

The debate about religion, evolution and the autonomy of

nature began in earnest with the publication in 1798 of Thomas Malthus' *Essay on the Principle of Population*. (Darwin's *On the Origin of Species by Means of Natural Selection* was not published until 1859.) Malthus held that population growth was bound to outstrip food production, resulting in periodic famine. (Population, unchecked, was bound to grow geometrically while at best the food supply could only grow arithmetically.) This was the basis for the doctrine of the survival of the fittest that emerged later.

Wm. Paley, a contemporary of Malthus and, like Malthus, an Anglican cleric, is credited with laying the theological foundations for reductionism. In the tradition of Descartes, Paley observed only the glory of God in the wonders of Creation as illuminated by science. His Natural Theology reassured those who felt their universe threatened by the new science that their world was in good hands, and that scientific discovery would only magnify the power and glory of the Creator. Nevertheless, during the latter half of the 19th century the relationship between science and theology changed, as secularism sought to make the claims of theology so abstract that they could not come into conflict with the discoveries of science.

The doctrine of the survival of the fittest, while popularly attributed to Malthus and/or Darwin, was actually put forward by of one of Darwin's contemporaries, Herbert Spencer, whose extremist interpretation of Malthus became the foundation of social Darwinism, and later, socio-biology.

Like Malthus, Darwin did not view his work as antagonistic to theology or the church, and while the "controversy in the 19th century between science and theology was very heated indeed... at another level the protagonists in that debate were in fundamental agreement. They were fighting over the best ways of rationalizing the same set of assumptions about the existing order".[117] In other words, they were fighting over what was to be the balance of power. (Think about the use of that dreadful phrase 'level playing field' in current discussions about international trade.)

As science assumed an increasingly autonomous orientation, the theologians attempted to maintain that all was well. The final result was not, however, what they would have wished. In retrospect, we could say of the first half of the 19th century that the church baptized and then confirmed Science, and Science, like an adolescent, then left the church, empowered and filled with pride. The church, for its part, had given over any critical relationship to Science: "the view of God changed from a natural theology of harmony in nature and society . . . to a Deity identified with the self-acting laws of nature. The latter were laws of progress through struggle. . . Science did not replace God: God became identified with the laws of nature."[118]

In the meantime, the practitioners of Science were not content to be confined to the laboratories of the universities. They had ventured forth into the commercial realm of applied science, technology, and were finding their rewards not in the blessings of the church, but in the gains of the marketplace.

Spencer's theory of the survival of the fittest, "became a rationale for unfettered capitalism, imperialism, and racism".[119] There is a strong argument to be made that British imperialism and the class structure of capitalism both owe a profound debt of gratitude not only to Adam Smith, but to Malthus, Paley, and the other Natural Theologians of the 19th century who provided the rationalization so necessary to the maintenance of social order in the face of exploitation. The Social Darwinists became the missionaries of capitalism, extolling the benefits of what, to them, was necessity. That the spread of the market economy required the force of the state was not a deterrent to their enthusiasm, just as today gigantic state subsidies to the corporate sector are no deterrent to the proclamation of the gospel of free enterprise. On the other side, all attempts at reform of inequities and injustices could be dismissed as being in defiance of Nature and her laws.

There is little practical difference between yielding to the laws of Nature and saying that 'it's all in the genes'. Either way, it is our lot in life to find and accept our place in the natural order of things. Science devotes itself to illuminating this natural order while technology is the inevitable expression of our efforts to organize our daily life according to the natural laws. Hence the union of Science and Technology that is so widely propagated today. God, if God exists, has been marginalized to the role of therapist, or solace in the face of the Inevitable, for which God, too, is responsible as the Creator of these iron laws. Thus the church is not to meddle in politics, economics, or science. It is to be content with debates on sexual mores and morality rather than the life and death issues of an economic system which, while ravaging Creation, increases the wealth and power of an elite at the expense of those it deprives.

> If one accepts biological determinism, nothing need be changed, for what falls in the realm of necessity falls outside the realm of justice. The issue of justice arises only when there is choice.[120]

DETERMINISM

Although the emergence of micro-biology and genetic engineering in the last decade has reinforced the determinism of 19th century social Darwinism, it is also spawning new visions and interpretations of the character of the universe, interpretations that are at last challenging the reductionist model of what is scientifically and socially observed and experienced. Science, attempting to gain a more profound understanding of the 'laws of nature', is offering other paradigms. One such paradigm is the 'self-organising' or 'process' system:

> Perhaps the most crucial feature of self-organising systems is what mathematicians call nonlinearity. For 300 years, scientists have largely been preoccupied with linear systems. . . . A linear system is said to be nothing more than the sum of its parts. . . . By contrast, a nonlinear system is more than the sum of its parts. . . . In reality, all physical systems are nonlinear, but they may behave in an approximately linear way when close to equilibrium.
>
> Traditionally, scientists tended to treat complex systems as annoying aberrations. Nonlinear systems are harder to study than linear ones. By focusing attention on simple linear systems, science developed a strongly reductionist flavour. . .
>
> We are beginning to see complexity as a natural state of affairs, rather than as an aberration.[121]

COMPLEXITY

If reductionism results in linear science, which pursues simplification, then complexity must be a sign of failure to get to the truth. If the process is complex, then it cannot be scientific. The food system pursues this logic: polyculture is reduced to monoculture; the mixed farm becomes specialised; the art of feeding livestock, or the earth, or our own babies, is reduced to a scientific formula determined *outside* of the system in which it is to be utilized. Shaver Poultry in Cambridge, Ontario, regularly calculates the most economical feed ration for its chicks wherever they are, from the Philippines to Africa, dispatching the advice electronically. Cargill will be happy to advise farmers of which feed is best for their animals according to the formulas worked out in its corporate lab many miles away, if not in another country. In the same manner, Nestlé or Meade Johnson will provide the most profitable (to them) infant formula to a woman anywhere in the world.

Nevertheless, ecologically, the survival of the fittest requires diversity and complexity. Life processes depend on the constant interaction between organism and environment (text and context), and on each being changed by the other in this dialectical process. Over-adaptation and simplification lead to the graveyard, as the organism becomes over-specialized and unable to relate in a healthy manner with its changing environment. As an editorial in the U.S. journal *Science* put it: "Some of our crop varieties require human assistance for survival."[122]

For all its claims to being scientific, and rational, the global food system has become irrational, regressive and highly vulnerable. There has been a steady overpowering of diversity and complexity by the technology of simplification and uniformity, despite the consequences.

Since biological survival and human community depend on complexity and diversity, we must begin to rethink the paradigms of our food system, and its principles of organization and behaviour.

CHAPTER 13

REVERSING THE LOGIC

In previous chapters I have described the logic of our industrial political economy, using the food system as an example. The forms of our food system, from the computer and the supermarket to biotechnology, the Green Revolution, and capital intensive monoculture, are all expressions of Cartesian reductionist philosophy coupled with social Darwinist science. We are told that it all adds up to Progress. And if you will only work hard and restructure your economy, personal and national, according to their dictates, then you too – or maybe your grandchildren – can enjoy prosperity and long life!

Those who benefit well from the current political economy and its food system would like us all to believe that we inhabit, if not the best of all worlds, then the only one possible. This was true before the collapse of the Soviet model of industrial society and is even more so now. Capitalism, with its industrial-corporate ideology, now feels secure in expressing a high degree of triumphalism – "I told you so." This attitude is reflected in the all too frequent refrain, We (Canada/the United States) have the most productive, most abundant and safest food supply in the world. "We produce the highest quality and most efficient meats in the world," read a letter to *Meat & Poultry* magazine.

But it is hard to accept the dogma that our system works when there were estimated to be more than two million people, including 800,000 children, using more than 400 food banks across Canada in 1993. In the United States, by March, 1993, the number of Americans participating in the federal food stamp program had risen to more than 27 million, about ten percent of the population.

The other side of the coin, naturally, is that there are vested interests served by the food banks: about 70% of Canadian food-bank donations come from food manufacturers and distributors, while it is estimated that two-thirds of all U.S. food stamp spending – more than $30 billion is budgeted for 1994 – goes back to food distributors and retailers.

Given the relentlessly increasing figures for North America, and the malnutrition and deprivation in those countries forced to follow the advice of the World Bank to modernise their economies, it does not seem reasonable to suggest that our system works. As long as there is a single hungry child, we must admit that the Market Economy does not work. The measure of justice is not how well the rich and powerful are served, but how well the weakest and most vulnerable members of the society are served.

It is not a lack of food that is the problem, as is clear by the money the governments of the northern Market Economy countries are prepared to spend to dispose of their surplus food (it is called 'trade wars' and 'export subsidies'). The problem is distribution, or rather the lack of functional distribution systems.

Envisioning alternatives is usually dismissed as utopian, but there is nothing more utopian than the idea that our system is adequate, or just, and that if we just carry on with it, its deficiencies will somehow be overcome. If we do reject the infinite projection of our present food system into the future, then we must imagine and implement alternatives now. But how to conceive of alternatives?

What better way to begin than to turn inside out the principles that don't work, or that work fine but for the wrong goal. Distancing, uniformity (or monoculture) and continuous flow seem to work fine as short-term principles for capital accumulation and the centralization of control. They do *not* work as principles for a sustainable, equitable and locally controlled food system.

Let us then reverse or invert the logic of distancing, uniformity and continuous flow. What we get is: *proximity*, *diversity* and *balance*.

PROXIMITY

The principle of proximity is simple: food should be consumed as close to the point and condition of production as possible. Maximum nutritional quality, maximum food security, maximum energy efficiency, and maximum return to those who contribute most to the food production process can be achieved in this way. Proximity has historically been simply a fact of life for most people, and breastfeeding, of course, is the epitome of proximity in the food system.

Another way of describing proximity is to say that the closer the food source is to the consumer, the less *money* is required for nutrition. An economic system that seeks to maximize the amount of money that can be made out of anything will pursue the logic of distancing, not proximity. Under the logic of proximity, there is very limited opportunity for chemical, mechanical, technological, or speculative intervention, since the objective is to minimize, not maximize, cash flow.

Fortunately, we are beginning to become aware of the extent to which distancing obscures from our vision and understanding the impact or fall-out of our food system. The ecological consequences of clearing rain forests for short-term cheap beef production, the consequences of over-fishing with deep-sea factory-freezer trawlers, the erosion of land resulting from continuous corn production, and the pollution of our sources of water through the gradual leaching of agricultural chemicals have been all but invisible to our short-sightedness. I remember vividly the gully in the hillside of continuous-corn beside the highway to town. Year by year it got deeper and wider and each year the farmer had to make larger detours around it to cultivate and plant his corn. Finally the farmer had to fill it with tons of rock to make the field usable, but no longer for corn. The fine clay soil was long gone downstream.

Proximity makes it difficult to avoid or obscure the consequences of what we do, whether it is the production and disposal of garbage or the overuse and pollution of water sources. For example, the overuse of surface water is obvious very quickly, while the overdrawing of water from an aquifer hundreds of feet below ground will not be apparent for some time. Cubans are aware that if they draw too much water from the aquifer under their island the sea water will enter the aquifer, making the watersource unusable. In contrast, the water table under Saudi Arabia is dropping at a rate of up to 45 metres per year in some places, with 92% of that water used for irrigating the desert in order to produce wheat while their water source is increasingly contaminated with sea water.

In the same way, water pollution from surface run-off of manure will be apparent very quickly, while the pollution from subtle agro-toxins may not be apparent for years. The irrigation of crops can be a form of distancing, the distance being overland through long pipes so that those who benefit in the short term are not aware that the lake is going dry. The alternative is better management of the water that is nearby, and this may require a transformation in the way we see the world.[123]

During the 1988 drought a prairie grain farmer explained to me how there used to be sloughs and water holes on the land his grandfather broke, but surface water came to be defined as a challenge to be overcome in order to accommodate the larger and larger equipment in use and the drive to increase productivity. The sloughs and wet holes – the natural reservoirs – had fallen into the same category as weeds, a nuisance to gotten rid of and a competitor for the land needed to grow a crop.

The summer of 1993, with the awesome flooding of the Mississippi River and the rivers feeding it, offers the same lesson on a grander scale. Seeking to gain control over the rivers, and seeking to maximize production in the short term, for years the settlers, farmers, and the U.S. Army Corps of Engineers sought to confine the rivers behind higher and higher levees. The land behind the levees could then be farmed and towns built. Control and production were the winners – but only for a while. When the rivers rose beyond any previously recorded levels – levels they never reached earlier because they would cover their flood plains at a certain point – and broke through the levees, it was a disaster. But this 'disaster' also brought with it a renewing of the land, for it was periodic flooding that built up the best farm land in the first place. This is as true of the Mississippi as of the Fraser River, the Ganges, the Amazon or the Nile!

Proximity obviously eliminates the demand that long-distance transportation makes on food for durability and shelf-life. Under a regime of proximity there is no need to design a tomato whose primary characteristic is durability. Nutrition can be the paramount concern. Proximity in potato production means growing varieties that are suitable to the local conditions and will provide maximum nutrition over a long harvest period, rather than being suitable for simultaneous harvesting and processing into frozen french fries for a continental market.

Proximity applied to other vegetables would mean the production of hardy indigenous crops like apples, carrots, and cole crops that store well in a good cold cellar without processing or packaging. Proximity means, as it does for me right now, going out to my garden to pick a delicious salad for dinner with a taste and tenderness that just can't survive distancing.

Of course, the more seriously proximity is taken as an organizing principle in general, the more impact it will have on demographics. Human settlement should be guided by the availability of food, as was the case historically for most people, rather than assuming that it is reasonable to haul food thousands of kilometres overland, or to fly it by jet halfway around the world, to feed a population centre *because it is there*. This simply makes too many demands on the food itself and imposes too many distortions on the food system, as well as creating an attractive situation for highly centralized control.

We will have to seriously consider decentralizing human settlements rather than continuing to assume that our current limitless centralization is the only possible way we can live together. Accompanying this will have to be the repopulation or establishment of rural towns and villages. This, in turn, will raise the social question of what kinds of human settlements we really want and what kinds are really sustainable. Food will have to be reintegrated into culture instead of marginalized as commodity.

The requirement that all cities produce 50% or more of their vegetable requirements within their city limits would have drastic and healthy consequences. It would have parallel consequences for those areas of the world presently under duress to produce and sell food to us so that we can continue to live as we do. If we were to grow much more of our own food near to home, then farm labourers, landless peasants, and peasant farmers around the world would stand a better chance of being able to feed themselves and their own communities. Brazilian peasants would not be removed from their arable fields and forced onto marginal hill or forested land that should not be cultivated just so some transnational corporation can grow soybeans for export to feed European cattle. Neither would cassava be grown in Thailand to produce tapioca for export to Europe as a high-protein feed supplement for livestock by a TNC such as Cargill.

Proximity is no cure-all, but in conjunction with other principles such as diversity and balance, would require both a radical transformation of the present North American food system and a radically different appreciation of human community. It would also provide society with more meaningful challenges than inventing new technologies to marginalize people and increase the distance between us and our food sources.

DIVERSITY

The pursuit of genetic diversity combined with the criterion of proximity would eliminate a great many pseudo-diverse items from the supermarket shelves while increasing the varieties of locally and regionally grown produce. Instead of two or three varieties of apples, there might be ten, with at least one of them a traditional variety that stores well until spring. The apple tree in our front yard on the farm was at least a century old. Its apples were not fit to eat until after a good hard frost. Picked then, they would keep at the top of our cellar stairs until early spring, when the rhubarb was ready to pick.

At the same time such practices would increase our appreciation of traditional polyculture and historic methods of food production while increasing the stock of genetic resources that are essential to a healthy food system and a healthy ecology.

Reductionist logic has greatly eroded our understanding of how processes and relationships create the conditions of community and ecology. Scientifically designed baby formula administered with a plastic bottle with a rubber nipple is no substitute for a mother's breast, with its intimate mix of physical, immunological and emotional elements. Starting life with a bottle and no cuddling probably has an effect similar to that of eating all your meals at a stand-up counter in a subway station.

Fits and starts, trial and error might better describe the unfolding of life and the development of its web than any linear notion of progress. Thus a fungus will send out its 'tentacles' in all directions until some of them touch a food source. Then it will withdraw its other exploratory probes and concentrate all of them on the food source. "Its collective organization and indeterminate growth allow it the best of all worlds by switching between sometimes radically different developmental pathways to suit different tasks."[124]

Have you ever watched pole beans send out their stems in search of light and support? Mine are now all over the tomatoes, the fence, and the bicycle shed!

> Organic chemistry in life is the outcome of a very long evolution, and it represents a highly restricted assemblage of compounds; incompatible compounds have been eliminated. In my opinion, an organic compound which does not now occur in living things has to be regarded as an evolutionary reject. Simply put, somewhere down the line a few billion years ago, perhaps some living cell got it into its head to synthesize dioxin and has never been heard from since. You need to regard the products of the petrochemical industry as evolutionary misfits and therefore very likely to be incompatible with the chemistry of living things.[125]

In a culture of superficiality, we seem to have substituted numbers for reality. Success is measured by cash flow, and diversity is measured in terms of how many different packaged goods can be produced out of identical raw materials or the least number of genes. It's called 'product differentiation'.

If reductionist logic were the truth, then reality, as we have noted, could be determined by sheer enumeration. The voting lists would tell you everything there is to know about a village or a city. But we know that is not true. In a large city, knowing that it is three kilometres from point A to point B tells you very little about how long it actually takes to get there by car or public transit, though it may give you a fair idea of how long by foot or bicycle. That is because there are so many other factors that have to be accounted for. In the same fashion, knowing that you planted 60,000 seeds will tell you just that, not that you will harvest 60,000 plants. There are a great many other factors that must be considered along the way, which is why the food-for-profit system seeks control through monoculture and the reduction of variables by means of industrialization.

While reductionist logic seeks to minimize variables, the result of the apparent stability achieved in, say, a plant population, is vulnerability. The greater the uniformity, the greater the vulnerability, the greater the dependency, the greater the insecurity. If the fans are not turned on at the right time in the chicken barn, a catastrophe will result. Chickens are not normally so dependent. If hybrid corn does not receive the right amount of the required pesticides and fertilizer, or a new bug wanders by, the whole crop is at risk because there is no diversity. If a bug strikes one, it strikes all in a monoculture.

A few years ago the Canadian Agricultural Chemicals Association changed its name to the Crop Protection Institute of Canada. Public distrust of chemicals and chemical agriculture was growing, and 'crop protection' was a more comforting idea. But the name change also signalled the increasing dependency of industrial agricultural crops on *protection*. No longer able to make their way in the natural world on the basis of their own strengths, industrial crops are dependent on an army of external interventions for their survival. In the case of agricultural chemicals, dependency has grown so extreme that the protection fails: 'hostile' bugs develop their own defenses in the form of immunity to the chemicals which are supposed to be protecting the plants. The chemical companies respond by designing plants capable of tolerating higher levels of pesticide or tolerating other pesticides to which the bugs are not yet immune.

A sustainable food system must reduce its dependency on

external supports to a minimum, and this can be achieved by maximizing diversity so that the food system as a whole is inter-dependent. Genetic diversity is the basis of a healthy population, and it provides the resources to respond to and interact with a constantly changing environment. If one variety succumbs, there will be another that won't, and a new resistance will be acquired. Besides, if you are producing food for your own family, you want to plant at different times and with different varieties to extend both the season and the pleasure.

Ecological agriculture in a system marked by proximity will be labour intensive, but it will also require a great diversity of human talents. Farms, and farming communities, will need to include a diversity of people of widely varying ages and physical abilities. The structure should ensure the everyone has time to think about and enjoy what they are doing.

The recognition of diversity as the basis of a healthy popula-tion would demand the reverse of the processes at work in our food system. We would know that we could not export what worked for us as the answer to a problem elsewhere. We would seek to expand the genetic base of our nutrition and look for het-erogeneity rather than uniformity. But this would be not only in genetic resources. The same logic would apply to processing in a decentralized system, and to the ways of preserving and dis-tributing food. If diversity is of any significance, then the least desirable way to organize our food supply is to centralize the con-trol over it into the hands of five or six mega-corporations.

BALANCE

A system seeks balance, like the sea water entering the aquifer under Cuba. When a hole for a fence post is dug in saturated ground, the hole will quickly fill with water and mud if the fence post is not quickly put in and the hole filled.

The idea of balance can also be observed in the determina-tion of plants and animals to reproduce themselves. If a hayfield is left to mature and go to seed, the plants then die back, having fulfilled their purpose. In a temperate climate the cycle is an-nual. If livestock are introduced, however, the plants will be grazed before they reach the seeding stage and then will continue to grow, trying to reach that stage again. Cutting a field for hay will produce the same results. However, if the natural annual cycle is interfered with, then responsibility must be taken for maintaining the balance. Thus if the livestock do not deposit their manure directly on pasture, then the farmer removing the hay will have to either return the manure to the ground later or replenish the resource in some other way, such as crop rotation.

Balance, which implies equity, is a prerequisite to sustainability. In the case of a sustainable and just food system, the balance must exist between those who grow the food and those who prepare it, those who distribute it, and those who eat it. There must be some balance between the resources used to produce the food and the replenishing of those resources. Linear processes are incapable of balance. "Continuous flow" is not the logic of a sustainable or just system, since it implies uni-directional movement. Phosphate rock mined and processed in Florida and shipped to Ontario, applied to farm land along with herbicides produced from Alberta oil in Windsor, Ontario, in order to grow corn that is then shipped to Nova Scotia to feed livestock that is shipped back to Montreal, does not add up to a balanced system. (I'm not making this up!) In the same way, there is no balance in a food system that requires its primary producers, as a rule, to live on a fraction of the income that is appropriated *out of the same system* by the chief executives and senior managers of the corporations that produce the agricultural inputs or process and distribute the food, or of Agriculture Canada or the USDA.

There is a perverse logic in the traditional antipathy of farmers towards unionized food processing plant workers or grain handlers. Perhaps farmers, wedded to an ideology of rugged individualism, resent the corporate strength of the unionized workers who may succeed through collective bargaining in getting an adequate wage. But those same farmers, perhaps because they have been indoctrinated to devalue their labour and to see themselves as businessmen, seem less concerned about the salaries of corporate management, or the profits made by the food companies. In other words, there is a characteristic *imbalance* in the allocation of return to labour in the linear food system, and this ought to be challenged by those who are the primary victims of the system.

An unjust, imbalanced system cannot be maintained without life-denying coercion and ecological violence. In many places this force takes the form of death squads which seek to maintain sufficient fear among a deprived population that they will not try to take over the lands that are being withheld from sustenance production – usually in order to produce cash crops for export, with the support of a government that seeks to preserve its privileges. It may also be complying with the demands of international finance (IMF/World Bank) to repay the debts incurred in the construction of the unjust, imbalanced system in the first place.

This is why the issue of privatization cannot be avoided. The essence of private property is the right and the ability to exclude others from the use or enjoyment of that property. Inequities and inequalities are far more easily maintained in a privatized culture than in a cooperative and genuinely balanced economy.

CHAPTER 14

SELF-RELIANT
FOOD SYSTEMS

It is not enough to leave the discussion of a just and sustainable food system resting on the logic of proximity, diversity and balance. We must consider the characteristics of a self-reliant food system incorporating these principles. The real fruits of our labour should be the development of human communities based on ecological sustainability and economic justice.

Self-reliance does not mean isolation or autonomy. It simply means relying primarily on those people with whom one lives from day to day and on the resources at hand, rather than being dependent on outsiders and external resources. It means carrying on external economic relations on the basis of equity and mutuality, not exploitation. Self-sufficiency, on the other hand, can be described as an attempt to be self-contained and independent, or autonomous.

BIO-REGIONALISM

Self-reliance requires, *a priori*, a working definition of *self*. In the linear corporate food system we have been describing, the self is a single unit, one piece of the system like any other piece: the self is a consumer or a worker, a means to a profit, without context. In a self-reliant, just, and sustainable food system, the self is defined in a real and specific geographic and biological context.

We all live somewhere in particular. This may seem a rather

obvious statement, but our present industrial food system is built on the assumption that we just live somewhere in general, with no particular context. Biology and geography are viewed simply as alienated natural resources to be exploited. A sustainable food system, by contrast, is by definition rooted in a particular ecology, a particular bio-region, and since these are all different, there will be many different food systems, even though they may share many common features.

The nation-state is still considered the basic unit of an economy, even though very few nation-states bear any more than a casual or accidental relationship to a bio-region. Many nation-states are larger than any one bio-region, and by their very structure and size overpower or simply exclude any internal bio-regionalism. Both Canada and the United States are good examples of this. Cuba, on the other hand, or Saltspring Island near Vancouver, might be considered bio-regions, while Japan might be considered a federation of several bio-regions conforming with the islands.

Rivers have always been arteries of societies, the thoroughfare around or along which communities have been built. Yet imperialism has almost always chosen rivers as boundary lines because they offer one of the few lines of demarcation that can be easily identified. If territory is to be defended, it helps to be able to tell the army where it is. Similarly commerce, left to follow its own particular interests, will locate around a lake, or on a coastline, not in the middle of a landmass. The reason is simple: water is the cheapest and most sustainable means of transportation.

There are natural, geographical ways of describing bio-regions, but it is less by their boundaries, which militarily may well be exasperatingly vague, than by their character. For example, the Great Plains of North America does not have clear boundaries that conform to those drawn up using the Mississippi River as a border. Nor does the political boundary of the 49th parallel bear any natural relationship to the Great Plains. Nor do the political divisions of the maritime provinces of Canada and the U.S.A. – New Brunswick, Maine, and Nova Scotia – bear much resemblance to the natural boundaries of the region. (Prince Edward Island and Newfoundland have to be considered separately because as islands, each is primarily its own bio-region before it is anything else.) The mountain-limited Pacific Northwest of North America constitutes a bio-region which includes British Columbia and some of Alberta as well as much of Washington state and even Oregon.

Bio-regionalism is not the same as continentalism. There is little hope of ecologically sound or geographically based economies in the political units of the size and diversity of the U.S.A., Canada, or the European Community. It is just as necessary to draw political boundaries around sustainable regions as to recognize that bio-regions cross political boundaries. The political map of Canada, the U.S.A., Brazil and many other countries would have to change drastically.

Bringing about such political change is obviously dependent on a radical change in the ruling political and economic forces. I am not proposing a political program here; only trying to establish the guidelines for self-reliance, particularly with regard to food, upon which such a change would have to be based.

There is nothing magic about bio-regions. It is simply that if one is going to base an economy, and a culture, on material reality rather than political or ideological abstractions, then one has to begin with a description and assessment of that material base.

> My favourite 'map' of the world is a composite satellite representation enhanced to emphasize topography and water. While vividly conveying the character of regions, and the significance of water or its absence, this 'map' does not indicate any political jurisdictions. It, and not the romantic, ethereal satellite picture of the globe as 'spaceship earth', should be the beginning of our thinking about where we dwell on the face of the earth.

Such criteria, however, bring us into immediate conflict with current population policies or practices. In the Market Economy it is expected that either people will move to where there are jobs, or industry will move to where there is cheap labour. It would be a radical departure from recent tradition if people moved to where they could feed themselves rather than to where they could sell their labour or the product of their labour.

Also essential to an ecological economy is a common sense of place (proximity) and the possibility of face-to-face communication. The village coffee shop may be the bedrock of democracy and sustainability.

One of the most visible and violent consequences of the industrialization of the food system in North America has been its effect on rural communities, including both infrastructure and population. The closing down of rail branch lines and grain elevators, milk routes and machinery dealers, schools and community services, referred to as 'rationalization' in current political jargon, has destroyed the viability of rural communities from coast to coast. Given the values of the Market Economy and the primacy it gives to the accumulation of capital, this is perfectly logical, but it runs counter to any notion of sustainability. While individual farm bankruptcy is bad, the failure of a community is even more devastating since it eliminates the context within which personal grief can be borne and shared and within which a different life can be nurtured. But even without putting it in such extreme terms, the isolation imposed on farming people by the current industrial, capital intensive system makes it both unattractive and dehumanizing. Farm children know this very well, and while they may feel real regret, they choose not to carry on on the farm, not because they do not like the work, but because they cannot tolerate the isolation and lack of community.

Clearly, then, any move towards bio-regionalism and sustainability must involve a deliberate population policy: a policy of re-population of rural communities. This may mean establishing new rural communities that are bio-regionally based rather than rebuilding communities that were situated according to the dictates of the railways or foreign commercial interests and not according to the needs of the land and the people.

There is little new in all this. In other lands and at other times, people have lived, and continue to live, in villages while working the surrounding land. While there have been both good and bad reasons for this, the pattern remains a sound one. But given the expectations people are now raised with, both good and bad, the isolated village is not enough. A good public transportation system that can provide access to larger centres with the cultural and intellectual resources that require a larger population base is both reasonable and necessary. While we may have convinced ourselves that the private automobile provides maximum freedom of movement, it does so only for those of certain ages and physical abilities, and then only at very high cost. Universal accessibility, meaning children and seniors, disabled and able-bodied, without regard to income, should be the criterion of public transportation just as it should be for nutrition.

It may, in fact, be appropriate that the rail lines are being abandoned, if only to show how badly they are needed, though perhaps organized and built to sustain a healthy society rather than to export its resources.

TRADE

Self-reliance, as we have noted, is not the same as self-sufficiency. While it may be possible to achieve a high level of food self-sufficiency in some locations, for reasons of cultural and social diversity and experience it may not be desirable. We are left, then, to consider the question of the nature of non-dependent, equitable economic relations between regions.

In the current ideological climate, which stresses the importance of organizing an economy for the purposes of export, a national economy is measured by its 'balance of trade'. But it is advantage, not balance, that is sought.

Trade is built on reciprocity and equity, and should be regarded as a function of communities, a social activity. Export, on the contrary, is a narrowly economic and political activity based on advantage and taking advantage; getting more than giving, as discussed in Chapter 9. The ideology behind export is growth; the purpose of an economy is defined as growth, and once internal markets are saturated, the only alternative for growth is via exports. The economists rationalize this with the dogma of 'comparative advantage', which says we will all be better off if we each produce what we can produce most efficiently. Today this may mean that the country with the lowest environmental standards should have a lot of pulp mills (like Nova Scotia), or a country with the lowest wages should have only labour intensive industries, like vegetable production in Mexico.

Trade follows different rules, its purpose being to expand diversity and extend mutual support, not to make the Gross National Product bigger. For example, trade between the Maritime region (of Canada and the U.S.) and the Caribbean could be a trade in potatoes, cole-crops and meat in exchange for tropical fruits, sugar and coffee. Or fish, a high-value product, could be traded between the Maritime region and inland industrial regions for tools and equipment (if the industrial harvesting of fish for export had not destroyed the fish stocks). Trade between bio-regions could mean trading Prairie grains for Ontario (or Minnesota) fruits and vegetables, or prairie range beef (or buffalo) for Florida oranges.

Trade, however, should never be the primary purpose of an economy, and nowhere is this more apparent than with food. The rule should be: feed the family and trade the leftovers; not, produce all you can and export all you can and keep your fingers crossed that there will be something left over for the family.

INCLUSIVE ACCOUNTING

A third aspect of self-reliance must be inclusive accounting, that is, accounting that includes all aspects of the economy considered over a long time. On a bio-regional basis, this means that resource depletion, labour exploitation, land degradation and water pollution, as well as all costs of infrastructure, must be accounted for. Contemporary accounting practices, reflecting and serving the logic of corporate capitalism, endeavour to externalize as many costs as possible, assigning them to either future generations, the public purse, or people lying outside their jurisdiction. Contemporary accounting practices thus negate the principle of full-cost or balanced accounting.

A pulp-mill which obtains publicly-subsidized electrical power, which utilizes and pollutes a public water supply, which pays less for stumpage, or for wood, than the full cost of obtaining that wood and reproducing the forest, is engaged in fraudulent accounting when these factors are externalized and do not appear on the corporate books as part of the costs of doing business.

The same thing holds true for farming and fishing. Factory

freezer-trawlers that overfish, thereby reducing the future fish stocks, must be charged for the cost of rebuilding the fish stocks. The social costs for the coastal villages that are deprived of their economic base in the meantime must also be included in the costs of doing business as a freezer-trawler, just as the soil losses and pollution resulting from crop monoculture must be charged as costs against the value of the crop.

In the same way, the unpaid wages of farm families and peasant labour must be factored into the cost of exported food. If the wages of the farm worker are not very close to those of the industrial worker who eats the food produced by that labour, the full cost of that food is not being paid, regardless of claims about comparative advantage.

In a bio-regional self-reliant food economy, all costs will be accounted for, not only the costs of sustainable production, but the costs of community. This will require a very different conception of accounting than that used for corporate tax purposes. Sustainability and long-term viability are simply not possible if real costs are externalized and left unaccounted for.

SUSTAINABILITY

Self-reliance requires sustainability. It cannot be assumed that fuelwood can be obtained outside the region once all the trees are gone at home. Self-reliance is the antithesis of export monoculture and dependency on imported food or agricultural inputs.

Sustainability means that there is no time limit to the economy or its accounting. Sustainable food production means that present production is not being obtained at the expense of future production. It also means that the system is alive and dynamic, like biology itself, not static, like monoculture. A sustainable food system is an equation in which there may be continuous substitution of one factor for another or increasing some while decreasing others. Fish species and food crops themselves may vary as other factors vary – such as long-term weather patterns, water levels, population pressures and deliberate or natural selection of species and varieties – not only from place to place but from generation to generation.

Sustainability also means that the resources called upon, or used, are renewed by the very process that calls upon them. Quite simply, if we are going to eat the progeny of a cow, then provision must also be made for the reproduction of that cow. If cereal crops are to be eaten, sufficient seed must be saved for replanting the crop next season.

Biological sustainability, like any economy, requires diversity. All organisms, and an economy is an expression of a population of organisms, require genetic diversity if the species is to be able to evolve with the evolving environment.

The so-called comparative advantage of monoculture is deceptive: it is has no future of its own. The external imposition of uniformity, whether to make harvesting easier, storage possible, or to facilitate corporate management, will exact its price of vulnerability and dependency. Being biologically static, designed to be dependent on external inputs like 'crop protection agents' and irrigation, unable to propagate itself reliably, and subject to all sorts of attacks for which it has few internal defenses, monoculture would soon pass away if left to its own devices.

To be sustainable, a system must be organic, that is, based on what occurs naturally within the local ecosystem. This means relying on the natural systems that have evolved over very long periods of time, during which organisms and components have interacted and reproduced on a continuing basis without depending on foreign or imported inputs, including engineered genes.

To describe a self-reliant food system as organic is simply to observe that what is non-organic, that is, introduced from outside the natural cycle, generally does not contribute to the health of the organism. The human body has to filter out and dispose of all the foreign matter that is introduced into its nutrient intake for purposes other than to feed the body, like the residues, however minute, from the application of agro-toxins.

A SELF-RELIANT FOOD ECONOMY

All of these factors can be combined in a self-reliant food system that is organically, bio-regionally, and community based. It will mean seasonality in foods, more labour input in production and processing, and greater genetic diversity coupled with much less superficial diversity. Instead of following the centralizing and destructive logic of industrial capitalist food, this food system will follow the decentralizing and integrating logic of diversity and interaction and the nurturing of biological and human communities.

This will mean smaller production units, smaller and more locally designed equipment, and the recycling of nutrients and organic matter, from water to manure and garbage. It will also mean a vastly reduced role, if any, for transnational corporations, whether chemical companies, grain traders or food manufacturers. It will mean the break-up of the vast food processing and distributing conglomerates now operating, with processing and packaging reduced to minimal levels as the whole food system is decentralized and localized.

Fruits and vegetables are most nutritious when they are fresh-picked. They have no choice but to deteriorate rapidly, since once harvested they are living organisms removed from their life-support systems. The most direct route, the least distance, to the final eater is the best route.

CHAPTER 15

DOWN TO EARTH

The Market Economy culture, with its technological and social determinism, is now so widespread and so deeply entrenched that it is hard to conceive of things being otherwise. The assumption that an economy, to deliver the goods, has to be based on greed and individualism appears to gain strength daily even in the face of its failures. The language of profit, efficiency and competition spreads through the media and distorts our vocabulary so that it is difficult to even find the words through which a different vision might be expressed.

While we recognize the deepening ecological crisis, our sense of alienation from the creation that sustains us ensnares us in a debilitating fatalism. Although we have profound myths, histories and ancient visions to draw upon, our imagination appears to have atrophied and our nerve withered.

To envision and pursue radical alternatives to the monoculture market economy, alternatives that will meet the requirements of ecological sustainability, human community, and Biblical faith, is not utopian. It is utopian, however, to think that we can solve the problems of the growing destruction of Creation, increasing hunger and deprivation, and deepening concentration of wealth and power in the hands of a tiny fraction of the world's people, with more debt, more technology, more oppression, and yet more exhortation to be competitive and productive.

In this book I have deliberately worked at two levels: theory and concrete example. When moving into the future, the same dialectic is essential. Taking small, specific steps toward an inclusive economy of food will at the same time nurture the vision that directs those steps. We cannot wait for a revolution to begin creating a new society: too much life is already being destroyed and too many options eliminated, as witness the destruction of rainforest and the loss of genetic diversity. The revolution begins with the ability to imagine a different future, and is carried out in the creation of new economies and societies.

EXPRESSIONS OF PROXIMITY

When I wrote the first edition of this book, there were few 'expressions of proximity' to point to. Times have changed. In the past four years farmers' markets have bloomed across the continent. Local bakeries making 'real' bread and 'organic' grocery stores can now be found in increasing numbers. Most significant, as expressions of proximity that also move toward the decommodification of food, are the CSA farms taking shape everywhere. CSA still stands for Community Supported Agriculture in many places, but Community Shared Agriculture seems to be taking over the initials.

The principle of the CSA is simple, as Farmer Dan points out in Chapter 6: a group of people become supporters of, or sharers in, a farm. It's as simple as that. It is also, in practice, a radical departure from almost every other form of economic organization to be found in agriculture today, at least in those parts of the world where industrial market monoculture has become dominant.

Community Shared Agriculture may begin with a farmer who wants to farm in a sustainable manner and recognizes the necessity of breaking out of the dominant system of exploitation. Or it may begin with a group of people who want high quality fresh food that is locally grown. However the 'consumers' and the farmer get together, the result is a shared enterprise: a farm in which the 'consumers' buy a share in the farm crop for an agreed upon percentage of the produce of the farm. These sharers also buy a share in the risk of growing the crop. If it is too cold for the tomatoes and peppers to do well, they may get more cole crops and potatoes, as was the case on many farms in 1992. If the crop fails, the loss is shared by all, not just the farmer. After all, the simple logic goes, the farmer is not responsible for the weather. By the same token, if the crop is good, the sharers may find themselves giving food away or preserving large quantities.

It's a simple philosophy, though in execution it is anything but simple. The work, like the crop and the risk, are shared. The farm year may well begin in the fall when harvest is over, with planning for the coming year. Maybe there are only ten sharers and this is just the beginning of the enterprise, or there may be two hundred sharers organized by neighbourhoods in the city. In any case, the land has to be prepared, the amounts and kinds of crops that are to be grown have to agreed upon, and the finances have to be settled. Maybe the sharers feel that the farmer's income is not adequate – reflecting their increased awareness of what intensive farming is about – and that the share price should be raised. Or maybe the sharers got too much food and they need more members. Then maybe there is a mid-winter pot-luck or dance to be planned because everyone has enjoyed the experience so much they want to get together socially before spring.

In the spring the farmer may organize some work days – rock-picking, seed bed preparation, or maybe even building a cold-cellar for the root crops and potatoes. After all, the point is to become as self-reliant as possible, at least in those foods that can be locally grown. And what is being discovered is that far more can be grown locally than most people, farmers included, ever imagined. It seems that the farmers who are willing to make this break with tradition in how they 'market' their produce are also willing – and usually eager – to break with tradition in many other ways.

Not only are there experiments with the diversity of crops that can be grown, but also with cold-frames and greenhouses, drip irrigation, raised-beds and composting. It goes almost without saying that almost all the farms are organic in method, that is, not using synthetic fertilizers and agro-toxins and seeking to build up the land through careful use of compost, crop rotation, companion planting, and so on. After all, the purpose is to provide healthy food for healthy people in a healthy community.

While virtually all CSAs are organic in method, few are certified as such or feel the need to be certified. In fact, there is a
mounting feeling that organic certification simply sets organic
food up to be incorporated into the dominant system as 'niche'
products. Besides, everyone says, when you know your farmer,
and can see where your food is coming from and how it is grown,
certification by some outside body is irrelevant. Clearly this is
one of the direct benefits of proximity.

The advantages of the CSA structure, in addition to those
already indicated, are that the farmers can get free of a lot of
dependencies. If the shares are at least partially paid at the beginning of the year, the farmer will not have to go to the bank and
borrow to put the crop in. Not only is the risk shared, but there
is no money leaving the farm or the community in the form of
interest payments. In minimizing other customary expenses for
fertilizer and chemicals, a lot more money is kept in the community. This continues throughout the year, of course, as the
money spent on produce stays in the community instead of flow-
ing out to California or Florida, or to corporate farms in Mexico,
or to retailers' head offices in Toronto or Germany.

The most radical aspect of community shared agriculture,
however, is the decommodification of food that occurs in the process. Sharers do not get, and pay for, so many pounds or kilos of
this or that. They get a share in what the farm produces. There
is no direct dollar value placed on the food, though it is not all
that difficult to figure it out afterward if one feels the need to.
The social relations between sharers and farmer are not those of
bargain hunters and commodity producer. (The singular 'farmer'
is used here for convenience – most CSAs are family farms or
involve a number of people in the farm enterprise itself.) The
common experience is that what both farmers and sharers get is
community instead of commodities.[126]

FARMERS' MARKETS

There is nothing new about farmers' markets. They probably can
be said to have a history going back to the first farmer who took
a few sacks of rice to the village square to peddle. In fact, farmers

markets, and farmers' roadside stands, have a more or less universal and timeless quality. Yet they all but disappeared from North America under the onslaught of modern processing and packaging, trucking, refrigeration and supermarkets during the past 40 years.

But they did not disappear altogether. Toronto's St. Lawrence Market (established in 1803), the market in Fredericton, New Brunswick, the famous market in Kitchener, Ontario (established in 1839), and others maintained their faithful clientele and kept the idea alive. Not everyone forgot the quality and pleasure that proximity could bring, and when farm finances got bad enough, farmers began to think twice about all the middlemen they were supporting. The idea of keeping more of what the final consumer is paying, while providing better quality, remains attractive.

In contrast to CSA, however, farmers' markets are not a radical proposition; they do not challenge the notion of food as commodity. The farmer grows what she thinks will sell, and the only 'contract' with the consumer is at the point of sale, where money and goods change hands. But this crucial difference does not detract from the attractiveness and utility of farmers' markets.

The growth in farmers' markets in Ontario is indicative of what is happening across the continent. In 1989 there were 60 farmers' markets in Ontario, and by 1993 there were 120. Curiously, the organizing initiative is coming from the community, not the farmers. Of the 60 new markets in Ontario, only two were farmer-initiated. And, as anyone who has visited a farmers' market knows, local crafts are always part of it – about 20%, in fact.

Those active in organizing farmers' markets say that what attracts people to them and keeps them coming back is the fresh local produce and the socializing; the same dominant values that motivate the CSAs. For the farmers it is the social activity – "There's more to the market than just selling my stuff" is the way one vendor put it – and the opportunity to sell directly to the public and keep a high percentage of the returns (stall fees for most markets are minimal).[127]

LOCAL BAKERIES

A lot of baked goods are sold at farmers' markets, of course, but since they are almost always open only one day a week, there is need for fresh bread on other days. In Winnipeg, a group of women used to get together every Saturday to bake bread for their families. When the neighbourhood bakery closed, they asked themselves, why not take it over? With the backing of neighbours and a church group some of them belonged to, they bought the bakery and began producing baked goods from local organically grown grains. The whole grain is ground daily in a small mill right at the front of the bakery, and as a result their breads – and their famous cinnamon buns – have a quality that cannot be achieved with industrially produced flour. (The wheat germ, which is oily, has to be removed in commercial whole wheat flour so that the flour will not go rancid.) When the flour is used the same day, all the goodness and flavour is still there in the grain and in the bread. One has to try whole wheat bread made with freshly ground wheat to know what proximity can produce. Right from opening day, the Tall Grass Prairie Bread Company has been a social and business success, exceeding the wildest dreams of its initiators.[128]

UNIVERSAL ACCESS TO NUTRITION

It is strange how we have come to regard as normal and reasonable the notion that the only way to eat is to first buy food at a store. We don't start life this way, and it is often a matter of years before we learn how to function properly as customers in the food system. We have to be taught (some might say brain-washed) to be accomplices in the crime of capital accumulation through the necessity of eating.

If we were to be consistent and the Market Economy universal, we might carry with us little air meters, so we could pay for the air we require. It would be a bit complicated, because we would have to have accounts with 'owners' of the air in every jurisdiction through which we might pass. Truly a challenge to the electronics and information processing engineers! But buying our basic nutrition, in the form of commodities, is no less absurd, though it does accurately reflect the ethics of an economy which measures success in terms of accumulated capital and value in terms of price.

Being alive is more than simply making and spending money, and so we must consider how we can make it possible to think of our lives differently. The provision of, or allowance for, the minimal requirements of air, water, and food for everybody is a commonsense beginning. The issue is universal access rather than market access. Applied to a food system, this would simply mean that the economy of nursing mother and baby would be taken as normative, not exceptional. (The manufacturers of infant formula, baby foods, and now 'weaning foods' have waged a determined campaign against breast feeding in order to enlarge their market while subverting a 'subsistence' economy.)

There are many ways one can imagine organizing the production and distribution of food to ensure that every person receives what they require as members of the society. Children do not make a decision to be born. We bring them into the world, and they remain our responsibility. In a sense we have recognized this in Canada through our medicare system with its principle of universal access. Yet basic health care, in the form of good nutrition, remains in the competitive Market Economy. This contradiction could be overcome by extending the already accepted logic of preventive health care to the provision of food. If our socialized medicine included nutrition, among the ancillary benefits would certainly be the reduction of our sick-care costs and an improvement in the well-being of Canadian farmers.

PRESCRIPTION FOOD

For a start, it ought to be possible for anyone who is ill because they are malnourished to get a prescription for food, just as they would get a prescription for a drug if that is what they needed. If such an idea seems utopian, ask the drug companies if they think prescribing drugs under medicare is a bad idea. The big food companies might love the idea of prescribing food if the public would pay for it.

If generic drugs are a good idea, then so is generic food. So when prescribing, the health professionals could stipulate clean, unprocessed food, and they could ensure that the mark-up would be minimal by simply setting ceiling prices for food based on full costs of production.

If the supply of clean, generic, just plain food is inadequate, the health authority could then seek to contract with farmers directly to provide the quantity and quality of food required. This food would then be available in a clinic without charge to those advised by the health professional to eat better.

Probably it would not be long before the healthy/wealthy people realized that they were being discriminated against and began to seek the same quality food. They might insist that they had as much right to the public or socialized food as the sick people, and of course they would be right.

EATING PLASTIC: THE FOOD CARD

This idea could be carried further. The technology is all in place for us to be able to introduce a Food Card system of basic food allocation. Quite simply, every person responsible for feeding themselves (and others) would be issued a card like their health card or bank card. This card would be encoded, like every other card, but the information would be about food: how many people were eating off that card, whether there were special requirements, etc. The card holder would then simply go to the nearest participating supermarket and 'buy' their groceries. At the checkout, the card would be scanned, and then the groceries, and then the card again. The weekly allowance of staple foods would be charged to the public program, while extras and non-food items would be paid for at the checkout. Such a system would ensure that everyone got what they needed, but no more. They would be free to buy, at the same time, whatever else they wanted or needed, paying for it in the normal fashion. The allowance limits set in the card would virtually eliminate fraud or profiteering.

Since good health cannot be achieved with sick food, and recognizing that food allergies are an increasing problem, we would want to ensure that the food in such a health-care system is also healthy. The production of healthy food would mean, in practice, the production of organic food, food produced without artificial fertilizers, pesticides, herbicides, preservatives, etc. It would mean even more than that, because even with the best clean soil, one cannot grow clean produce like lettuce in an environment like Toronto's: the air is too polluted. This does not mean the requirement is impossible, just that it is more radical than we might initially think.

Just as we have found it necessary to protect the public interest by legislating standards for drugs, we could also legislate standards for food quality, or at least for the food that goes through the public nutrition sector. At the same time, society as a whole would have to pay the primary producers (who should be comparable to the medical profession in public esteem and monetary remuneration) to produce the kind and quality of food we require. This need not raise the cost of food to the society, since this approach would eliminate much costly processing, packaging and advertising, to say nothing of costly agricultural inputs like agro-toxins and synthetic fertilizers.

In accordance with the principle of proximity, the production of clean food should be carried out as close to the population centres eating it as possible. Reducing the present absurd expense of long-distance overland trucking would free financial resources that could be shifted to primary production and local distribution of healthy food.

CONTRADICTIONS

Each of the strategies described above have both drawbacks and advantages. Any of them, or all of them in any mix, could be a beginning. Which one is initially pursued will obviously need to depend on local circumstances and leadership. But whichever strategy is taken up, there should be a clear understanding of which issues it does or does not address.

For example, prescription food and the food card address the issue of universal access to basic nutrition, and they may address both food quality and proximity, but they do so individualistically. Both CSA and farmers' markets are strongly social, and address the questions of proximity and food quality, but they are not universally accessible. The significant difference between farmers' markets and CSAs is that the latter decommodifies food, while the former does not.

The most difficult issue to get a hold of is the role of the state, and/or state bureaucracy. Both the food card and prescription food scenarios require the state (government at some level) and utilize state power for their execution, whereas both CSAs and farmers' markets can proceed with little or no state or bureaucratic knowledge, much less interference or control.

	Proximity	Food Quality	Social	Decommodify	Univ. Access	State Involv.
Food Card	?	?	no	yes	yes	yes
Prescription	?	?	no	yes	yes	yes
Farm. Mkt.	yes	yes	yes	no	no	no
CSA	yes	yes	yes	yes	no	no
Bakery	yes	yes	?	no	no	no

Not surprisingly, the principle of diversity says there is no one answer to the question of a decommodified and sustainable food system. Any one of the above approaches can be a good beginning. The requirement is that we begin where we are, with who we are, while recognizing that we may be working on only one piece of the puzzle for now. Others must be encouraged to work on other pieces as well.

OWNERSHIP

We still have many romantic images of the family farm, but it is essential that we consider what they really are, and whether or not they ever really existed. It may be that 'the family farm' is another of those alienating dreams that render us impotent in the face of the forces taking control of the food system. As we rethink the food system, the rapid decline in the number of family farms could be viewed as an opportunity rather than a disaster, encouraging us to recognize that the private ownership of the means of production, including land, may itself be a major cause of the destruction of those elements of the family farm that we value. The profound need for human community, and the real practical need for security of tenure on the land, may compel us to create what are, for this culture, novel forms of farm organization, such as co-operatives and land trusts.

As a Salvadorean peasant said, returning to her home after being a refugee in Honduras, "It's stupid to look after your land alone. If you get sick it doesn't get harvested. When we work together, if one person gets sick the land is still looked after."

There are three basic land issues: ownership, stewardship, and security of tenure.

Farmers feel very strongly that they have to *own* the land they farm, even though, in both the U.S. and Canada, they rent or lease more than a third of all farmland they currently work.

The dominant culture of North America has long asserted that the only real security for agriculture lies in the private ownership of land and there is, for good reason, a profound distrust of absentee ownership, which includes ownership by the state. But this attitude has been and continues to be very costly for farmers.

For example: when we needed to obtain more land for our farm in Nova Scotia, we were delighted that the provincial government had just introduced a program of landbanking. Under this program we were able to make a deal with a retiring farmer whereby the Province would buy the land and lease it to us at a rate commensurate with its agricultural value. We were assured of security of tenure and a fair agricultural rent for as long as we wanted (which turned out to be about 12 years). However, no sooner was this program in place than the Federation of Agriculture began complaining that farmers had to have an option to purchase, which was not in the program we had been happy to take advantage of. (We wanted to work the land, not own it.) So the government responded in a reasonable fashion: they changed the program so that there was an option to buy and changed the rental basis from the agricultural value of the land to the market value. This effectively doubled the rent. Fortunately for us, the government honoured our rental agreement under the original terms as long as we farmed, but the farm organization destroyed a very good program simply because of the ideological commitment to the 'right' to own land.

It is precisely this ideological commitment which is bankrupting farms and destroying the family farm. The interest on debt against farm land, built up in the 70s and early 80s, is the major cause of farm failure in North America, coupled with commodity prices too low to carry this debt. And while individual farmers may still hold legal title to the land, the fact is that their mortgages, and thus their security, are held by outside interests, whether the Farm Credit Corporation, a bank, a provincial lending authority or a credit union. In the United States the insurance companies are among the major land-owners. In many cases, the farmer now has less security of tenure than medieval serfs had: "The medieval serf had been almost the opposite of a property owner: the land had owned *him*. He could not move freely from place to place, and yet he had inalienable rights to the piece of land to which he was attached."[129]

The net financial effect of this situation on the farm economy is that the farm has to be refinanced every generation. This constitutes an unsustainable drain on the entire rural economy, not just the farm, and it means that real control does not rest finally in the farmers' hands or in the rural community, but in the corporate boardrooms of the metropolis. Paying interest on a farm mortgage is little different from paying for agricultural chemicals. The money leaves the farm and rural economy and eventually inflates the value of urban land and housing.

LAND TRUSTS

One way of holding land so that security of tenure can be achieved would be to have all agricultural land held in some form of public trust, which could be very local. Then the rules of tenure would become a public responsibility rather than being the prerogative of urban capital as is the case now. This would force a clarification of roles and responsibilities: those people who wanted to farm could do so, with security of tenure contingent on their cultural practices and care of the land, and those who wanted to speculate would have to find another arena. Rent, if any, on the land being farmed could be geared to the value of the sustainable production of the land and paid into the local trust which might, in turn, provide a pension for the farmer. The responsibility of the community to the farmers would be to ensure an adequate living, including a pension, and the necessary social and economic infrastructure. Ecology, care of the earth, sustainability, all would then be the concern and responsibility of the whole community.

There is nothing novel, in fact, in this approach. It is gaining increasing acceptance and popularity as a way of conserving forests and ecological diversity around the world. Without even questioning the moral legitimacy of owning land, one can begin to de-commodify it by removing it from the market. A land trust can be private, like the Nature Conservancy, or it can be public, like the Saskatchewan land bank once was. And it could be private or public at any level. There is no reason a province or a municipality or a city could not be the land-holding unit. There is adequate precedent in our park system, which a great many people enjoy. (Not that there are no issues to be debated about the philosophy of park management, but at least those issues are in the public domain.) Also, there is no reason that farmers could not themselves form a trust, give or sell their land to the trust and then rent it back. The point is that there are many alternative ways of holding land. That so little thought has been given to these as viable options suggests that the issue is less practical than ideological. The development of a just and sustainable food system is going to require addressing both practical and ideological issues, and the very idea of being able to *own* land at all.

The native peoples of North America have never shared the capitalist concept of land ownership, and they have always understood their relationship to the land in spiritual terms. They are not alone in holding that the land simply cannot be owned. Even within European culture and history there have been different concepts of land ownership, and there is ample precedent, for example in the English 'strict laws' of the 19th century, for considering land ownership as a trust, requiring stewardship, not exploitation.

It was the practice of the English landed classes after the English civil war to deliberately tie their lands to their families through the legal instrument known as a strict settlement. The arrangement made the living recipient of rents into a mere tenant of his heir. Being perpetually only ever stewards for the next generation, the English landlord class prevented itself from taking a short-term view of land-use. Land had always to be passed to the heir in a condition at least as good as before.[130]

If we think about the possible ways of holding land as a common resource and a trust for future generations with stewardship and sustainability as the criteria of use, then we must also think of social structures and institutions that make this possible. As people experience the de-commodification of food through Community Shared Agriculture, it will become only logical for them to think about the de-commodification of the farm land. From buying shares in the farm crop to buying shares in the farm itself and setting it up as a community trust is a natural progression.

Stewardship of the land and sustainable agriculture require human labour. They demand a variety of work that makes it possible for men and women of all ages to participate in the working life of the farm and the community, as we noted in Chapter 13. From reforestation to composting, from seed conservation to food preservation, from cooperative building of community facilities to machinery repair, there should be work for all. Storytellers, teachers and healers will also be essential members of the new farm community. For teenagers, labour-intensive gardening might well be a more rewarding form of labour than stacking shelves in a supermarket or serving up pre-fabricated burgers at the local drive-in for minimum wage. Food could be restored to its rightful and necessary place in the centre of community cultural life through common labour as well as celebrations.

Our present industrial food system, pursuing the logic of distancing, has effectively alienated most people from any relationship to food other than that of consumers, a demeaning category. Any restructuring of the food system will have to overcome this degrading alienation. At the same time, if universal accessibility means that everyone is entitled to adequate nutrition as a member of the society, then everyone also has to take responsibility for the food system in the same way they have to take responsibility for their health.

FULFILLING THE BIBLICAL VISION

> Oh, come to the water, all you who are thirsty; though you have no money, come! Buy corn without money, and eat, and, at no cost, wine and milk.
> *Isaiah 55:1*

Earlier I set out my understanding of the Biblical vision of how we are to organize our economies and treat Creation if we intend to live together in peace. The *how* has to do with relationships and attitudes, and the Biblical insight is that we have to make these material, concrete. Our vision has to be incarnated, made flesh, in our economic arrangements.

We feed each other with bread, not a stone. This bread conveys our solidarity. To insist that nourishment – salvation – must be purchased is immoral and sinful. Restructuring the economy so that its purpose and function is to provide for the essential needs of all can best begin with the food system. The personal question is, do we seek justice and community, or power and wealth?

In the middle of our farmhouse kitchen was a round solid pine table. Anyone entering the house came directly into the kitchen and invariably sat down at the table. Being round, the table could accommodate many people, and it had no head place. Being in the kitchen, it was also the work-table for the kitchen economy. Food and community were inseparable. That table was the centre of our business and social gatherings as sheep farmers. It was also at that table that we held a weekly Bible study and Eucharist. Our children, those staying with us, and a neighbour or two were symbolic of the larger community and economy of which our farm was a part. There was always enough to eat, and there was always room for more at the table.

NOTES

(dates are given as day/month/year)

1. The old Massey Ferguson combine plant in Toronto was demolished in the mid-eighties and some of the land on which it stood "developed", though already a trust company that inhabited one of the new buildings has gone bankrupt. M-F itself became Varity Corporation and the M-F farm machinery subsidiary was recently sold to Agco, Inc. of the U.S., leaving four full-line farm, equipment companies operating in North America: Case International, John Deere, Ford New Holland, and Agco, which is really just a distributor.

2. Post acquired the ready-to-eat cereal business of RJR Nabisco and its 2.9% market share in January, 1993, for $450 million. – *M&B News*, 16/2/93

3. L. Curtain, *Food Market Commentary*, p.23, Sept. 1988, (Agriculture Canada, quarterly)

4. Jay Scott, tomato breeder at the U. of Florida – *The Packer*, 19/6/93

5. Dick Dawson, quoted in *Western Producer*, Nov. 17, 1988 (Saskatchewan Wheat Pool, Saskatoon, weekly)

6. G. Temple, *FOOD In Canada*, Nov/Dec. 1988 (MacLean-Hunter, Toronto, monthly)

7. *FOOD In Canada*, June 1987

8. *FOOD in Canada*, Oct. 1988

9. *Globe and Mail*, Toronto, 23/2/90 (daily)

10. *Milling & Baking News*, 20/8/91 (weekly, USA)

11. Wm. Cronon: **Nature's Metropolis, Chicago and the Great West**, Norton 1991, pp. 101-2

12. Cronon, ibid, p.145

13. Cronon, ibid, p.146

14. Exodus 16:13-21, **Jerusalem Bible**

15. Vandana Shiva, **The Violence of the Green Revolution**, Pluto, 1992

16. See Brewster Kneen, **The Rape of Canola**, NC Press, 1992, for an exemplary story of this process as it applies to rapeseed/canola.

17. Interview, 1986

18. Dan Morgan, **Merchants of Grain**, Penguin, 1980, p.86

19. Concentration in the North American Milling Industry: The ten largest U.S. milling companies

largest U.S. milling companies	No. of mills	wheat-durham-rye daily capacity, cwts
ConAgra, Inc	31	296,400
ADM Milling Co.	30	291,100
Cargill, Inc.	21	225,400
General Mills	8	76,600
Cereal Food Processors	9	69,800
Bay State Milling	8	66,100
Italgrani USA	2	39,300
Nabisco Brands	1	28,000
Amber Milling	2	32,000
Mennel Milling	4	22,700

source: 1993 Milling Directory & Buyer's Guide

20. *The Packer*, 5/6/93 (weekly, USA)

21. *ChemicalWeek*, 9/9/92

22. *The Packer*, 24/4/93, 29/5/93

23. *Report On Business Magazine*, 5/93 (monthly, Canada)

24. *Business Week*, 14/6/93 (weekly, USA)

25. *Canadian Grocer*, 1/92

26. composite

27. *The Packer*, 1/5/93

28. *Food in Canada*, 9/92

29. Company letter

30. *Milling & Baking News*, 9/2/93

31. *Milling & Baking News*, 4/5/93

32. *Canadian Grocer*, 2/91

33. *Globe & Mail*, 11/7/92

34. Jack Doyle's **Altered Harvest** Viking, 1985, contains a 48-page table of Agribusinesses and the Food Chain, giving investments in agriculture, genetics, and biotechnology research.

35. *Report on Business Magazine*, Aug. 1993

36. Canadian Franchise Association membership directory, 1993

37. *Land Stewardship Letter*, Stillwater, Minnesota, Fall, 1988

38. Statistics Canada

39. Herb Norry, "Farming as a Business" in **Farming and the Rural Community in Ontario**, T. Fuller, ed., Foundation for Rural Living, Toronto, 1985, p. 81

40. *New Scientist*, 17/12/88, (Britain, weekly)

41. See Chapter 2, "Apocalypse Cow" in **The New Why You Don't Need Meat**, Peter Cox, Bloomsbury, 1992

42. *Poultry Grower News*, #13, 4/93 (USA)

43. Interview, 1986

44. Jeremy Cherfas in *New Scientist*, 9/5/92

45. Doyle, op. cit., p.174

46. *Globe and Mail*, 29/2/88

47. Doyle, op. cit., p.176

48. Marc Lappé, **Broken Code, the Exploitation of DNA**, Sierra Club, 1984, p. 139; and, Omar Sattaur, "Native is Beautiful", *New Scientist*, 2/6/88

49. Seed Saver Exchange, R.R.3, Box 239, Decorah, Iowa 52101, USA; Heritage Seed Program, R.R.3, Uxbridge, Ontario, L9P 1R3, Canada

50. Vandana Shiva, interview, 1986

51. Jeremy Cherfas in *New Scientist*, 9/5/92

52. Jeremy Cherfas, ibid

53. Tom Murphy, "The Structural Transformation of New Brunswick Agriculture, 1951-1981", thesis, University of New Brunswick

54. See Jack Kloppenburg, **First The Seed**, Cambridge, 1988

55. Goodman, Sorj and Wilkinson, **From Farming to Biotechnology**, Basil Blackwell, 1987, p.34

56. Goodman et al, ibid, p.138

57. Goodman et al describe the transformation of agriculture in terms of what they call "substitutionism" and "appropriationism", the former applying to the output side of agricultural production and the latter to the input side:

Appropriationism: "the discontinuous but persistent undermining of discrete elements of the agricultural production process, their transformation into industrial activities, and their re-incorporation into agriculture as inputs." (p.2)

Substitutionism: "the industrial transformation of agriculture . . . through a series of partial, discontinuous appropriations of the rural labour and biological production processes (machines, fertilizers, hybrid seeds, fine chemicals, biotechnologies), and the parallel development of industrial substitutes for rural products." (p.2)

The essential first step of substitutionism in the food industry was to interpose mechanized industrial processing and manufacture between the source of field production and final consumption. Once this step had been taken, the rural form of the commodity and its constituents could then be modified and obscured, facilitating its treatment and presentation as an industrial product. (p.60)

To illustrate: Margarine is described as "the precursor of industrially fabricated foods" to illustrate this process of substitutionism. Margarine represents "the manufacture of an industrial substitute for a processed *rural* product, butter, using cheaper raw materials." (p. 69)

58. Farm Credit Corporation, 1992 Farm Survey

59. *Business Week*, 14/6/93

60. **Canadian Agriculture in the Seventies**, Report of the Federal Task Force on Agriculture, December 1969, Ottawa, p.9

61. FCC Farm Survey, 1992

62. *Canadian Grocer*, 12/88

63. Empire Co. Ltd. 1992 annual report – Empire owns Sobey's grocery stores

64. *The Packer*, 12/6/93

65. *Ontario Tater Times*, 13/9/90 (published by the Ontario Potato Growers' Marketing Board)

66. *Forbes*, 2/8/93 (weekly, USA)

67. See Kneen, **The Rape of Canola**, for a detailed description of this process.

68. Langdon Winner, **Autonomous Technology**, M.I.T. Press, 1977, and Langdon Winner, **The Whale and the Reactor**, Univ. of Chicago Press, 1986

69. Doyle, op. cit., p.222

70. Technical Manager, NutraSweet Co.

71. Jerry Mander, **In the Absence of the Sacred**, Sierra Club, 1992

72. *Science*, 11/11/88

73. *Canadian Grocer*, 11/1988

74. Sabine Häusler in *The Ecologist*, May/June, 1993

75. "Enclosure in Britain", *The Ecologist*, July/Aug. 1992

76. Bent, Schwaab, Conlin and Jeffery, **Intellectual Property Rights in Biotechnology Worldwide**, Stockton Press, 1987, p. 141

77. Bent et al, op. cit., p.139

78. Bent et al, op. cit. p.167

79. Alberta Pool Budget, 9/7/93

80. 1989 figure, in Susan George, **The Debt Boomerang**, Westview, 1992, p.10

81. In 1992 Canada exported $5.68 billion worth of grains and grain products out of a total of $12.13 billion in agricultural exports. Canada's total agricultural imports for the same year were valued at $8.54 billion, of which grain and grain products totalled only $.67 billion. On the other hand, Canada exported $0.55 billion worth of vegetables, fruit and nuts while importing $3.09 billion worth. For live animals (excluding poultry), red meats and other meat products, the figures were $2.82 billion for exports and $1.09 billion for imports.

82. The following indicates the relative size of these companies in 1992 revenues: Ciba-Geigy, $15.6 billion; Bayer, $26.4 b.; Sandoz, $10.2 b.;

Rhône-Poulenc, $15.4 b.; Cyanamid, $5.3 b.; DuPont $37.2 b.; BASF, $28.5 b.; ICI, $21.3 b.

83. *AgBiotechnology News*, 12/92

84. *AgBiotechnology News*, 2/93

85. Calgene vp Andrew Baum quoted in *Manitoba Co-operator*, 25/3/93

86. "Greek and medieval Christian thinkers . . . philosophized about the *oikonomia*, that is, the problem of organizing the *oikos* or household, the community of those who cooperate under one roof. In Roman law the household, under the 'father of the family', was the cell of social life, and the higher and more inclusive organizations both in ancient and medieval life were conceived on the analogy of the household." – E. Heimann, **History of Economic Doctrines**, Oxford, 1964, p. 22

87. Susan George, **The Debt Boomerang**, Westview, 1992 p.xv, also:

According to the OECD (Organisation for Economic Cooperation and Development, Paris) between 1982 and 1990, total resource flows to developing countries amounted to $927 billion. . . Much of this inflow was not in the form of grants but was rather new debt. . . During the same 1982-1990 period, developing countries remitted *in debt service alone* $1345 billion (interest and principal) to the creditor countries. For a true picture of resource flows, one would have to add many other South-to-North outflows such as royalties, dividends, repatriated profits, underpaid raw materials and the like. (George, op. cit., p. xv)

88. Unicef, **State of the World's Children 1993**, p.57

89. Quoted by Robert Heilbroner in **The Essential Adam Smith**, Norton, 1986, p. 265

90. in Heilbroner, op. cit., p.294

91. in Heilbroner, op. cit., p.297

92. Unicef, **State of the World's Children 1993**, p.57

93. Karl Polanyi, **The Great Transformation**, Beacon Press, 1957, p. 117

94. A.C. Nielson Co. Canada

95. *Globe & Mail*, 3/8/93

96. Edward Yoxen, **The Gene Business**, Harper and Row, 1983, p.142; see also Anderson, Levy and Morrison, **Rice Science and Development Politics**, Oxford, 1991, for a detailed and critical analysis of the development and work of the International Rice Research Institute.

97. in Heilbroner, op. cit., p.322

98. **Food 2000 – Global Policies for Sustainable Agriculture**, Zed, 1987, p.6

99. Richard Levins and Richard Lewontin, **The Dialectical Biologist**, Harvard, 1985, p.2

100. *New Scientist*, 24/7/93

101. Kempton Matte, interview, May 1987

102. Goodman et al, op. cit., p.96

103. Goodman et al, op. cit, p.138

104. *Globe & Mail*, 30/1/91; *Oils & Fats*, #5, 1992; *Fortune*, 28/6/93

105. David Waltner-Toews, however, is one of the majority who believe pasteurization is essential. See his **Food, Sex and Salmonella, The Risks of Environmental Intimacy**, NC, 1992

106. Doyle, op. cit., p.134

107. Richard Lewontin, Steven Rose and Leon Kamin, **Not In Our Genes**, Pantheon, 1987, p.167

108. Omar Sattaur, "Native is Beautiful", *New Scientist*, 22/6/88

109. Agriculture Canada Plant Industry Directorate communique, 28/7/93

110. ibid

111. from "Genetics of Disaster", *Journal of Environmental Quality*, Vol. 1 no. 3, 1972, quoted by Fowler and Mooney, **Shattering**, U. of Arizona, 1990 p.46

112. Calestous Juma, **The Gene Hunters**, Princeton 1989, p.14 – other estimates say that the world relies on only 30 plant species for about 95% of its food needs.

113. Cary Fowler and Pat Mooney, **Shattering**, Arizona, 1990, p.70

114. Corporate promotion, 1985, and interview with R. Hurnanen, 1988

115. Langdon Winner, **The Whale and the Reactor**, Chicago, 1986, p.5

116. Mander, op. cit., p.37

117. Robert Young, **Darwin's Metaphor**, Cambridge, 1895, p.191

118. Young, ibid, p.240

119. Walter Anderson, **To Govern Evolution**, Harcourt Brace Jovanivitch, 1987, p.56

120. Lewontin et al, op. cit., p.236

121. Paul Davies, "The Creative Cosmos", *New Scientist*, 17/12/87

122. *Science*, 6/5/88

123. See Marc Reisner, **Cadillac Desert**, Penguin, 1987, for a wonderful epic history of water in the west, and the war waged against both water and desert.

124. Alan Rayner, "Life in a Collective: Lessons from the Fungi", *New Scientist*, 19/11/88

125. Barry Commoner, *Science for the People*, March/April 1987

126. For more information about CSA, see *The Ram's Horn*, nos. 100, Dec. 1992, and 103, March 1993. (monthly) The Ram's Horn, 125 Highfield Rd., Toronto, Ontario M4L 2T9, Canada

127. For more information on farmers' markets in Ontario and elsewhere, contact Farmers' Markets Ontario, 75 Bayshore Rd., R.R. 4, Brighton, Ontario, K0K 1H0

128. Tall Grass Prairie Bread Co., 859 Westminster Ave., Winnipeg, Manitoba

129. Lewis Hyde, **The Gift**, Vintage, 1983, p. 121

130. Colin A. M. Duncan, "Lessons in Sustainability from English History" in **Global Perspectives on Agroecology and Sustainable Agricultural Systems**, edited by D. van Dusan and P. Allan, Univ. of California Press, 1988

BIBLIOGRAPHY

Anderson, Robt., Edwin Levy and Barrie Morrison, **Rice Science and Development Politics**, Cambridge, 1991

Bennett, Jon, with Susan George, **The Hunger Machine**, CBC, Toronto, 1987

Busch, Lawrence, Wm. B. Lacey, Jeffrey Burkhardt, and Laura Lacey, **Plants, Power, and Profit – Social, Economic, and Ethical Consequences of the New Biotechnologies**, Blackwell, 1991

Cronon, Wm., **Changes in the Land – Indians, Colonists, and the Ecology of New England**, Hill and Wang, New York, 1983

Cronon, Wm., **Nature's Metropolis – Chicago and the Great West**, Norton, 1991

Doyle, Jack, **Altered Harvest – Agriculture, Genetics, and the Fate of the World's Food Supply**, Viking, New York, 1985

Fowler, Cary, and Pat Mooney, **Shattering – Food, Politics, and the Loss of Genetic Diversity**, Arizona, 1990

Fukuoka, Masanobu: **One Straw Revolution**, Bantam New Age, 1985

George, Susan, and Nigel Paige, **Food for Beginners**, Writers and Readers Publishing Cooperative, London, 1982

George, Susan, **Ill Fares the Land – Essays on Food, Hunger, and Power**, Institute for Policy Studies, Washington, 1984

George, Susan, **The Debt Boomerang – How Third World Debt Harms Us All**, Westview, 1992

Goodman, David, Bernardo Sorj & John Wilkinson, **From Farming to Biotechnology**, Basil Blackwell, Oxford, 1987

Hyde, Lewis, **The Gift: Imagination and the Erotic Life of Property**, Vintage Books, 1983

Kloppenburg, J.R., **First the Seed - The Political Economy of Plant Biotechnology**, 1492-2000, Cambridge, 1988

Kramer, Mark, **Three Farms - Making Milk, Meat and Money from the American Soil**, Bantam 1981, Harvard 1987

Levins, Richard, & Richard Lewontin, **The Dialectical Biologist**, Harvard University Press, Cambridge, Mass., 1985

Kneen, Brewster, **Trading Up: How Cargill, the World's Largest Grain Company, is Changing Canadian Agriculture**, NC, 1990

Kneen, Brewster, **The Rape of Canola**, NC, 1992

Lewontin, R.C., Steven Rose and Leon Kamin, **Not In Our Genes, Biology, Ideology, and Human Nature**, Pantheon Books, New York, 1984

Morgan, Dan, **Merchants of Grain**, Penguin, 1980

Nabhan, Gary Paul, **Enduring Seeds - Native American Agriculture and Wild Plant Conservation**, North Point Press, 1989

Pacey, Arnold, **The Culture of Technology**, MIT Press, Cambridge, 1983

Palmer, Gabrielle, **The Politics of Breastfeeding**, Pandora, 1989

Reisner, Marc, **Cadillac Desert - The American West and its Disappearing Water**, Penguin, 1987, 1993

Shiva, Vandana, **The Violence of the Green Revolution**, Zed/Third World Network, 1991

Winner, Langdon, **Autonomous Technology**, MIT Press, Cambridge, 1977

Winner, Langdon, **The Whale and the Reactor, A Search for Limits in an Era of High Technology**, Univ. of Chicago Press, 1986

Young, Robert M., **Darwin's Metaphor, Nature's Place in Victorian Culture**, Cambridge Univ. Press, Cambridge, 1985

Yoxen, Edward, **The Gene Business, Who Should Control Biology?**, Harper and Row, New York, 1983

INDEX

THE RAM'S HORN, published by Brewster and Cathleen Kneen since 1981, is billed as 'a monthly newsletter of food system analysis'. Published in a highly readable, 8-page format, eleven times a year, The Ram's Horn is an important source of data and ongoing discussion of the issues raised in **FROM LAND TO MOUTH** – from new developments in Science & Technology to emerging corporate strategies and activities, from seeds to CSAs.

Personal subscription: Can.$15/year in Canada, US$15 outside of Canada
Institutional subscription: Can.$25/year in Canada, US$25/year outside of Canada, payable to:

> THE RAM'S HORN
> 125 Highfield Road
> Toronto, Ontario, Canada
> M4L 2T9
> (416) 469-8414

Brewster Kneen is also the author of

TRADING UP:
How Cargill, the World's Largest Grain Company,
is Changing Canadian Agriculture, NC Press, 1990

and

THE RAPE OF CANOLA, NC Press, 1992